How to Find the Path to Your Destiny

By: Dana Marie Rivas

XULON PRESS

Xulon Press
2301 Lucien Way #415
Maitland, FL 32751
407.339.4217
www.xulonpress.com

© 2010 by Dana Marie Rivas

All rights reserved solely by the author. The author guarantees all contents are original and do not infringe upon the legal rights of any other person or work. No part of this book may be reproduced in any form without the permission of the author. The views expressed in this book are not necessarily those of the publisher.

Due to the changing nature of the Internet, if there are any web addresses, links, or URLs included in this manuscript, these may have been altered and may no longer be accessible. The views and opinions shared in this book belong solely to the author and do not necessarily reflect those of the publisher. The publisher therefore disclaims responsibility for the views or opinions expressed within the work.

Unless otherwise indicated, Scripture quotations taken from the New King James Version (NKJV). Copyright © 1982 by Thomas Nelson, Inc. Used by permission. All rights reserved.

Printed in the United States of America.

ISBN-13: 978-1-6121-5067-3

TABLE of CONTENTS

Chapter One:
The Situation 1

Chapter Two:
A New Day 17

Chapter Three:
A New You 49

Chapter Four:
The Connection 73

Chapter Five:
Let's Expose the Lies 87

Chapter Six:
The True Promise 125

Chapter Seven:
The Mourning Period 139

Chapter Eight:
Building Healthy Habits 145

Chapter Nine:
Tests and Trials 155

Chapter Ten:
The Victory 167

Chapter Eleven:
Journal 173

The Situation

I am going to tell you right off the bat whether this book is for you or not. If any of the following situations ring a bell for you... then read this book:

Are you wishing your life had more meaning...more purpose? Do you feel hopeless? When you think about your future do you see nothing, absolutely nothing, to get excited about–and that frightens you? Do you feel like if one more bad thing happens to you, you're going to lose it, and just go crazy? You can't take it anymore. You're frustrated, worn out, drained and disappointed with life. You feel like you just want to give up and throw in the towel. You're tired of trying different things and not getting anywhere. Do you feel trapped? Do you feel like you're supposed to have more or be more at this time in your life, but you're not making any progress? You're losing hope and running out of steam. Every day you tell yourself that you've got to do something to make a change...sign up for a class... make a career change...move...etc. But week after week ... year after year has gone by and nothing has changed. You're still in the same rut, feeling more and more miserable. Do you feel like maybe what you're doing in life right now, is not what you were meant to do in life or where you're supposed to be? Do you feel like everyone around you and life is just passing you by–while you're stuck spending countless hours each week, devoting the best hours of your day and all your time and energy on a life and in a situation, you now realize you were not meant for? And every day you're growing more and more anxious and desperate for a way out. You just want inner peace, passion, joy, and happiness to be in your life again?

Perhaps you've had your head buried in the books all your life–stuck in a library and in front of a desk. And now... your only moments of joy and sense of identity comes from showing off your intellectual superiority to others. Showing them that you know all the answers–and that you get all the A's – always trying to impress people with your educational awards and honors. You've been caught up in this internal obsession to get to that next level and to always achieve the best marks, so you'll feel that burst of joy and satisfaction when you get to the next rung on the corporate ladder or earn another degree or get that promotion or receive the good grades and you brag about it to all your family, friends, and acquaintances. But the satisfaction quickly fades, and you're left feeling empty.

Or perhaps... you are consumed by celebrity: Celebrity gossip, celebrity magazines, celebrity news, celebrity style, celebrity weight. Do you spend hours a day reading the celebrity tabloid magazines and talking with friends about what the celebrities are doing this week (as if you know them)? Do you spend all your money on clothes, purses, and makeup to look like and follow the trends that you see in the magazines and on TV? Do you spend a lot of your time fantasizing about or trying to get on reality TV? And now you're starting to get anxious because you're getting older and if you don't get on a show soon, you'll feel completely worthless. Do your only moments of joy and sense of identity depend on people commenting on how cute you look and that you should be on TV?

Or perhaps you're someone who struggles with constantly falling back into negative/unhealthy behaviors that you wish you could break free from once and for all? You might do well for a period, but then someone says something to you that gets you all irritated or something happens... and you're right back into it. You want to do the right thing and become a better, healthier person–for yourself and the people you care about, but something always seems to happen that drags you back to your old negative ways right when you feel like things are going so well. Whether it be drugs, alcohol, a shopping addiction, abusive behavior, porn, cutting... etc. Do you tell yourself before going out to a bar that you're only going to have 2 drinks and not stay out the whole night, so that you can get a good night's sleep and be functional the next day...for once? But the next thing you know it's 1:30am, you're 8 drinks in and trying to find out who's having an after party? Or do you eat "good" all day long–and you're so proud of yourself–thinking that maybe you'll actually lose those 2 pounds this week and then at the end of the day someone frustrates you so bad... the next thing you know you're on the couch devouring a large pepperoni pizza, a bag of potato chips, a tray of chocolate chip cookies, and then washing it all down with a tub of ice cream. Or do you tell yourself that you want to stop spending so much money each month and start trying to save... but then your favorite catalog comes to the house or you see something on QVC that you've been wanting for a long time... and it's on sale! Or you go to the mall just to buy one thing (and only if the price is right you tell yourself)...but then when you get there, there are so many cute outfits on display and so much that you don't have ... and you start to feel so good imagining how great it will feel to wear a new outfit to work on Monday and all the different outfits you'll be able to mix -n- match with what you currently have. You can't stop thinking about it... you almost must buy everything just to quite the thoughts in your mind so you can move on. You're riding high now on your way home from the Mall or immediately after placing your online purchases. Feeling powerful and proud of the great buys and amazing outfits you purchased and thinking about how good you're going to look in your new clothes… you can always start saving next month–you tell yourself. But then… next month, it happens again. Or do you struggle with an addiction or personal affliction that you can't pass off as "normal", so you try and hide it, secretively enduring the shame and personal struggle all on your own. I mean… on Monday morning at the office coffee machine, when someone asks you how you spent your weekend–a shopping addict or compulsive spender can say… "I went to the mall this weekend and spent way more then I wanted to because I'm supposed to be trying to save." This sounds kind of normal to the average person because we've all been there at some point. Splurged one weekend on items we didn't really need. However–only that person would know the truth deep down, that it's truly a bigger issue then it sounds and that it is really turning into an addiction that the person struggles with daily. But at least this person can share some of his/her struggles and still be accepted by mainstream. But one couldn't say… "Man–things got crazy this weekend. My family got into a big argument or I felt like no one was listening to me, so I began cutting again or used crack." Do you suffer in silence, fighting against the pull and desire toward negative, self-destructive actions? Have you gone several days or even months or years trying to be "normal", trying to "do right" and then one day something doesn't work out exactly how you envisioned it would–you become especially frustrated, tired, and irritable one day and that old familiar desire creeps into your mind and becomes your sole focus until you give in because the thought was burning a hole in your head? It was all you could think about and you felt like you were going to explode if you didn't give in. (As if a thought is more painful than the consequence of acting on the self-destructive desire.) Wow! That is how powerful thoughts are! I'm sure someone out there has had a problem with using drugs or dysfunctional behavior like exposing themselves in public and has successfully managed to stay clean for a while and maybe even promised loved ones that it would never happen again–but then one day that thought creeps in and creates an urge and a desire so strong that you'd rather live with the chance of getting arrested and/or kicked out of your home and not being able to function in society... rather than managing a small thought. But then... once you've crossed that line, and acted upon the thought, you just shrug your shoulders and say, "Oh well... it's too late now... already off the wagon... might as well jump right back into the old lifestyle and old behaviors headfirst." You figure you're just not good enough to change for the better. It's too hard. You can't do it. Then you wake up the next day feeling miserable, worthless, and disgusted with yourself because once again... you couldn't maintain the changes for good and your family is disgusted with you and has lost all hope for you too.

Or perhaps you struggle with bad habits, such as lying or speaking harshly and putting other people down when you get frustrated or angry or overwhelmed with all the things you need to get done. How many times have you told yourself, "This weekend I'm not going anywhere, I'm not doing anything? I'm just going to stay home and catch up on some sleep, get up early and start that new exercise program, grab a cup of coffee, pay some bills and go over some important papers I've been neglecting–organize the house a little, sign up for a class I need to take for work, update your resume, maybe go to church." And then the weekend comes along... Friday night a friend that you haven't seen in a while gives you a call and asks if you want to go to happy hour. You end up staying out for more than an hour. You wake up late Saturday afternoon, turn on the TV and there's just one good movie on after the other... before you know it... the sun is starting to go down. Then someone calls you to tell you it's their sons' birthday and they're having a little get together. You feel obligated to go–but you tell yourself before you leave that you're only going to stay for a little while. You try to leave the party a couple times but you're having a good time, and everyone convinces you to stay. You ate three hotdogs, two BIG pieces of cake, a ton of chips, beer, margaritas. You wake up late Sunday afternoon... most church services are over by now. You realize that you've got to do some laundry to have clothes for the work week and you need to go buy some groceries. The rest of the day you spend on Facebook... and now it's time to go to bed and get ready for another work week. Monday morning rolls around and you're disappointed in yourself because you did nothing that you told yourself you wanted to do–and this has been the cycle week... after week... after week. Has a loved one recently died or come to near death and now you've realized how short and fragile the gift of life is. That it is a gift and that you haven't maximized your life to your fullest potential. But now you want to. You want to contribute something to this world, but you're not quite sure what to do and where to begin? And to top it off... now you're beginning to realize... that after all these years... you've been following a path in life that isn't really you–that's not your destiny. And as a result, your life isn't giving you the joy and satisfaction that you envisioned it would at this stage in your life. You're feeling trapped, lost, disgusted, anxious, suffocating in this world–with no direction, no passion, no courage, no sense of purpose and no idea of what to do next. And with each year going by faster than the previous one–the thought of being stuck where you are right now for the rest of your life is depressing and wearing you out. Do you daydream about getting in your car or hoping on a bus one morning, leaving for work and never coming back? Starting a whole new life in a brand-new place where you can be different? Where you can be the person you were meant to be. Do you dream about winning the lottery, quitting your job, and moving to a remote island village... quitting life as you know it and starting over some place new? Are you feeling tired and beaten down by life? Is your mind constantly racing a million miles a minute from the time you wake-up until the time you fall asleep–trying to figure out what would be the best thing for you to do to get yourself out of this rut and to squelch that inner turmoil and those thoughts that just keeps building and building inside of you each day, burning a hole in your mind? Is your frustration level getting more and more intense every day because you feel deep down that you are meant to do something else with your life... something more... or go in a different direction with what you're currently doing–but you're growing weary of trying to figure out how to get "there", and you're losing hope. You just want peace of mind and want the inner struggle to be over so you can enjoy life.

Well... I'm here to tell you that that "something more", is out there for you, you just need to locate it. Locating "it" is easier said than done (As I think we've all experienced up to this point).

This is where this book comes in. There is a reason you haven't found "it" yet. Your enemy is hoping life will grind you into the ground before you reach your destiny and find that peace, prosperity, purpose, and joy in your life. Don't let that happen. There is a path that is waiting for you that leads to inner peace, passion, and purpose for your life. And this path is specifically designed just for you. Do you think maybe part of the reason you're not at peace and your life isn't full of passion is because you followed the plans and ideas laid out by others and society: all my friends were going to law school... all the other girls at school were taking those pills...everyone else has kids by now...everyone is buying those shoes and has the latest fashion...I'm supposed to have a big house by now... my teacher told me I wasn't smart enough and that I should choose another major.

Ok... so we've established that you're not satisfied with your current situation in life. You're feeling desperately unfulfilled. And, to make matters worse... you have no idea how to break out of this rut you're in. You don't even have a clear idea of what it is you're supposed to be doing with your life. What would make you feel at peace and content for the rest of your life? What would give you so much joy and make you feel so good about yourself that you would never go back to your negative/self-sabotaging/self-destructive ways. What is your destiny in life?

Doesn't it feel like the past few years have just flown by, and you can only recall them like a dream–in bits and pieces– and you're not quite sure which event came before what and which one was the major cause for your derailment from the right path you were supposed to take in life. What were those key decisions... or lack of decisions and direction, that got you stuck in this rut anyway? Are you full of anxiety because you're not sure how to break out of your current routine and get off the path you're currently on? But you're sure of one thing... Something deep within is compelling you, urgently pressing upon you, that there needs to be a change... and quickly. You've realized that you're longing for something more out of life...

for purpose... inner peace and contentment... a better you... the good life. "But how exactly do I find this," you ask yourself. How do you determine what path you should take in life?

I don't know about you... but no one in my life growing up ever taught me or talked to me about how to determine my purpose and destiny for my life. They certainly didn't teach this or even hint about this in any of the classes I took in school. Learning the difference between plant cells and animal cells is fascinating stuff to me but does that mean that that's my destined path in life? It's not even hinted at in those course catalogs that list all the majors offered in college or in those online tests that are meant to tell you what line of work you should go into. They should have warnings on those things: WARNING ** WARNING: Listening to the results of this test, a college course book, your parents, society, or friends when deciding what path to choose in life may lead to loss of joy, contentment, and inner peace. It should not be all about choosing a career or a path in life that is known to be high paying, recession proof, popular, glamorous, or because it was in an online article titled "Best Careers of the Year". No one can tell you what the best career choice for you is. They can be an additional resource for you, to tell you what's available out there and what a typical day may be like in a specific field. But we must try and keep the pressures and perceptions of the world from influencing our decisions. You'll have to continually analyze and re-evaluate your strengths, weaknesses, and personality traits all the time and make that decision of what path to travel and which turns to make for yourself. It should be about you, following your inner passions and following your inner voice no matter if it's popular today or not. It should be about what is right for you, where you fit best and what makes you vibrant and come alive with an inner passion. Just because a career is known to have high paying potential... that doesn't necessarily mean you are going to be paid well. Especially if you're miserable and hate the job or find the job hard to do, then you're going to find that you don't get promoted and get low performance ratings. And just because a career is known to be low paying, but it comes easily for you and you love it, and it makes you come alive with a creative passion that doesn't happen for others that do it, and it doesn't even feel like work to you. You might soar straight to the top and be one of the few high earners in that field. Working a job and choosing a career path (especially when one is young and just starting out), is more importantly about putting in an honest day's work and growing and maturing from the life lessons and personal awareness you learn along the way. Now I know your mind is racing these days... going a million miles a minute from the time you wake up in the morning (if you're even able to sleep at all)–anxiously analyzing all your options; Trying to figure out what "feels" right to you. And you feel like you need to figure it out quickly because of societal pressures to, "have it all", by this time in your life. So, you're frantically running through scenarios in your head, trying to figure out where you went wrong and what your next move should be. You're thinking "Should I be this, should I take this class, should I quit my job, should I see a therapist, should I dump my boyfriend, should I try that at home business, should I move to a new state and start over, should I break off this engagement, should I...". This is when many people just give up and settle for where they are in life, wherever they are, and whoever they're with–even though deep down they know they are destined for something greater. I guess this is because we get scared and insecure. A surfer who has been bitten by a shark once may not be as footloose and fancy free when he gets back in the water. If we step out and try to do something big with our lives–for example, allocating a lot of money on a business and then it fails–life bites us in the rear end... we too will be a little less footloose and fancy free when it comes to taking risks and trusting life. We don't want to appear to others as though we're unsure with the choices we make for ourselves in life; we're afraid to look like we've made a mistake or that we're going backwards in life too. So, the minute things get hard or someone laughs at us for trying to improve our life, we fold like a poker player with a pair of 5's going up against a full-house. But what if you hung in there and stayed persistent and persevered and two more 5's came down the river. People won't laugh then. Knowing which hands, you should stick with and persist with is the tough part though. And sometimes we've lived with our negative behavioral traits, feeling down, and depressed for so long that we can't even remember what it feels like to be free of anxiety and how to live without being miserable and sad all the time. That's how everyone knows you now, and how you know yourself. So out of fear of the unknown, or out of fear of failure, or fear of what others may say, and because of pride... people decide to settle for their bleak, disappointing life–never giving destiny another thought.

But sometimes it's better to swallow your pride and to take a few steps back in life and pause for a season to reassess your current situation and to force yourself to look at things from a different perspective, when you have more life experience and wisdom under your belt. How many of you have thought, "Man...I wish I could go back to high school or college now and start over, knowing what you know now and feeling how you feel about the decisions you made. What would you do differently? Choose a different major, participate in class and all the activities school had to offer, fully immerse yourself in the whole learning process, pay attention in class, take school more seriously, or never go out with a particular person? If I fall into a hot tub time machine and go back in time to high school as the person I am now–I wouldn't just do enough to get by... I would pay attention and fully engage myself in and participate to the max in every class and the whole school experience. I would get to know my teachers and other respectable adults like my Sunday school teachers and/or music and dance teachers and ask them to share their experiences and life lessons they have learned along the way. I would have minored in dance in school. I would've gotten involved in theater. I would have found a charity to help with and get involved in. I would have been more thankful and grateful for what I had and not such an ungrateful delinquent child because the situation could always be worse.

When we get a piece of fabric caught in the track of our zipper on our pants while rushing to get dressed to go out... initially we tug and tug and stubbornly tug some more... until finally we realize we can't keep going like this–we've got to stop and take the zipper back down to see where the problem is, assess the situation, take corrective action by cutting off the loose fabric strings that are caught in the zippers' teeth. After that... we have no more problems with the zipper on those pants again, which will save time and aggravation the next time around. So, it goes for life... if we had stopped and thought about it, corrected our actions and had done right the first half of our lives we wouldn't be so worn out and aggravated now. We wouldn't know the heart ache and stress and aggravation that weighs heavy on our minds now. But what if you did go back to school or you do start over some place new? What would you do? What is your guarantee that after you did all that and invested all those years and money into starting over that you're not going to end up miserable and disappointed and unfulfilled all over again? Just in a different miserable situation? What's your guarantee? I know that you just want to get out of this stormy life and onto smooth, calm waters as quickly as possible ... and out of desperation and the desire to relieve the pressure you're currently feeling as quickly as possible you want to do something now–now–NOW.

But don't just yet. Do you even trust yourself right now? I mean... you did get yourself into this mess.

Don't make any life changes that add to your plate right now. Lessen your obligations if anything. Do Not Add. If you get money back from your taxes and your cousin calls you about moving to Toledo and starting a small business...that's what I'm taking about... don't make any big/life changing decisions right now. If it's your job that's bringing you down and you're stuck doing something you can't stand, but you purchase a $700 car payment. Take a step back. Buy an old car–loose the car payment and start putting $500 a month into a savings account. Because if you decide to go in a new direction or make a drastic change in your life on your own right now, how do you know that it will squelch that inner turmoil?

Or would it lead to just making matters worse and get yourself deeper in a rut. And make you feel even more miserable and depressed because you'll feel like you've failed... yet again. Do you spend your days looking back on your life and analyzing all the decisions you've made over the years–all the twists and turns of your life–and find yourself wondering... what if? What if you had chosen to go to another school... what if you had never quit playing sports... what if you had taken that other job offer... what if you had stayed at your old job... what if you had quit smoking... what if you won the lottery... what if you had gotten that part in that movie... what if you had stuck to your instincts and done what you wanted to do despite what your parents said... what if you had gotten rid of that boyfriend the very first time your gut told you that he wasn't right for you... what if you had completed school... what if you had kept in touch with that guy... what if, what if, what if... stop it, stop it, STOP IT! Ok... ok yes... maybe if you hadn't given up on sports or if you had accepted that other job (who's employees all became millionaires) ... or whatever it is you're wishing you would've done differently–maybe you would be a world class athlete or in a better spot right now. Maybe you would be blissfully happy and content in life. But that was your destiny back then.

However, because of a few wrong choices and bad decisions–you veered off that path and missed out. I don't believe that that is it. That that was your only shot for a life full of destiny, purpose, passion, and inner peace and that now you must live the rest of your life in regret, uninspired, and unfulfilled. NO!

Just take a deep breath and hit pause on your life while we go through this book. By the time you work through the journal exercises in this book it will be clear what your next step should be. This book is designed to help lead you to identifying your destiny. And just knowing what your next step will be...I mean reeeeaallllly truly knowing for sure and not just having a hunch... even if it is several months away from happening–will begin to bring peace to your soul and contentment to your life.

Let's get down to it, shall we? The stars have realigned, the plates have shifted, the earth is spinning in a new direction. It is the dawning of a new day. There is a new destiny for you out there, and we're going to get you back on track so you can find it.

A New Day

Journal Exercise #1: Using the journal pages in the back of this book, write down the activities that you currently do, or did as a child, that made you come alive with passion and joy.

I'm talking about the kinds of activities that even if you were dead tired and could barely keep your eyes open–you'd wake up for. The kinds of activities that you'd get so focused on… the hours would just fly by. And you wish you didn't have to stop and go to bed or stop to go to work or school. Think back to your childhood. Take your time. It may take you several weeks or even months or a year to remember all those special activities that you enjoyed doing as a child. You might have forgotten substantial things. Look at old pictures… ask family members and friends what they remember you always doing as a kid…read comments from old report cards or job performance reviews. As you recall these memories–write them down in the journal pages provided for you in the back of this book.

Here are some questions to try and jog your memory:

- What were your very first answers when people asked you what you wanted to be when you grew up?
- Did you collect anything as a kid?
- What was it that fascinated you to the point that you collected it?

- What did you do when you were in the private sanctuary of your bedroom? Is that when you played dress up... or pretended to interview presidents in the mirror... or wrote music...or studied gray's anatomy...?
- What were your favorite toys to play with as a kid and why?
- What were your favorite books to read?
- If all your bills would be paid for you, and if you didn't have a mortgage or rental payment or a car payment what work or activities do you think you would choose to do?

Once you have a list of several activities; review the list and identify some common characteristics between some of the activities you've written down. Under the list, write down a few sentences about the common theme of some of these items. Maybe ask someone to tell you what they think the common factors are.

Now... going forward... anything new...any new club, any new job, any new hobby, any idea for a new business... etc., that someone suggests to you or you're thinking about adding to your life–compare it against this list. If it doesn't fall in line with the themes of your list, then dismiss it right away! Don't waste your emotional energy thinking another minute or daydreaming about it a second longer. Even if it's "supposed" to make you millions. For example, my list includes the following activities:

- Performing Dance Routines
- Climbing trees/hiking in the woods
- Collecting Nuts & Bolts
- Reading Nancy Drew Books

- Baking Cakes and Cookies and pretzels
- Playing Atari Video games trying to beat my high score
- Snow Skiing
- Watching Top Gun
- Researching and reading in the library
- Going on church retreats
- Going through my closet and seeing what new outfits I can put together from existing clothes.
- Building websites

My analysis of the common characteristics between my activities list is: Physically active, outdoor activities, hands-on, creative challenge, problem solving challenges, structured-focused short-term projects.

It might take you a while to complete your list. You might have forgotten some of the things you enjoyed doing as a child. Take your time. But as you remember certain activities, jot them down. I was in a home that was being remodeled one day, and out of instinct I picked up this shiny bolt and I felt excited suddenly, like I had made this great find and started imagining what could be built with it. I instinctively reached down and picked up this shiny bolt... and then suddenly, I remembered that I collected nuts and bolts, that I would find lying on the sides of the road when I was a kid. I had totally forgotten about this. Weird I know... but it's what I collected – don't judge me :)

Take a deep breath. Closing your eyes, hold one nostril shut while you inhale slowly for a count of 5, hold your other nostril shut while you exhale slowly for 5. Do it again! I am wheeling the iron curtain shut on your past right now! If you turn to go back to your past, you're just going to slam against that iron curtain and break your nose. You can only go forward now. We've pulled out from your past and written down the only things we'll need from that time of your life, the positive things that made you feel good and alive inside. That is all you'll need from your past–leave all the rest of it behind that iron curtain–leave all the pain, disappointments, and sad times back there.

> "Look to this day for it is life; the very life of life; for in its brief existence lay all the truths and realities of your existence: The bliss of growth, the glory of action, the splendor of achievement! For yesterday is but a dream and tomorrow is only a vision, but today well lived makes every yesterday a dream of happiness and every tomorrow a vision of hope; look well therefore to this day!"–Sanskrit

Journal Exercise #2: Beginning today–look at each day as a brand-new chance for you to create experiences of **bliss from growth**, **glory from action**, or **splendor from achievement**. And record these experiences in the Journal.

Do something right now that you've been putting off. Get up! Take action! Right now! Here are some ideas: update your resume, do 20 push-ups/20 sit-ups/50 jumping jacks, send a card or call a friend to let them know you're thinking about them, clean up that mess in the basement, hang those blinds that have been sitting in the corner for 6 months, enroll in that class, do a little reading for your job so you'll be on top of things Monday, or begin working on that paper for the class you're taking. I mean it. Put this book down now and go. Ok. Now that you're done... in the journal area in the back of this book, for this week check or circle either "Glory from action", "Bliss from growth" or "Splendor from achievement", and briefly describe the action, growth, or achievement you made, and describe the glory, bliss, or splendor you felt as a result. Pause for a moment here... and reeaaallllyyyy take in the bliss of the growth; the glory you felt from taking that action; or the splendor felt when you made that achievement. Each week make this a game you play with yourself to seek out and create opportunities of bliss from growth, glory from action, and splendor from achievement. Strive to have something to write down in your journal each week.

This will help to keep you looking forward and bring positive energy into your life and make you feel good about yourself. And this can help keep you from being too much in your head pondering things. Have you ever had an idea or suggestion at work that you hung onto and kept to yourself for weeks or even months ... and then finally when you brought it up in a meeting, and it was well received you felt relieved, powerful, productive, a part of something–I bet you stood a little taller and held your head a little higher and looked people in the eye more that day, right?... you felt glorious because you acted on your idea and on what you felt was right. So each week now, turn your journal to a new page and look forward to creating situations of bliss, glory and/or splendor. Do you need to have a tough conversation with your boss, co-worker, or family member that you have been putting off? Set that as an action for this week and just do it. Here are some other suggestions to start off with: Do you wonder why they call it Fat Tuesday? Do you know what the difference between Great Brittan and the United Kingdom is? What is fossil fuel as opposed to regular fuel? Have you forgotten what each branch of the government does or are you curious about what the entire constitution says, or who all those people are that signed the declaration of independence? Explore the bliss from growth you'll feel by gaining new knowledge. Are you the type of person that doesn't speak up when someone has offended or taken advantage of you because you don't want to be unlikable or rude? The next time someone offends you or says something you don't agree with–just think of it as an opportunity to fulfill this assignment and take action — speak up. Express calmly your thoughts and feelings about the situation and enjoy the glory and inner strength you'll feel from acting. Do you want to get a certification in your field? Each week your action can be studying practice tests and reading for this certification. Then one week you'll be able to check off the splendor from achievement category when you pass that certification. Make this a game you play each week with yourself to get at least one activity written down each week. It will help to keep you forward thinking and growing as a person. Because the wheels of time are in motion my friend–the tables have turned–you have awakened from your slumber–the earth has shifted–the stars are realigned–you are refocusing. There is a new destiny for your life, and it is just as great as the first one, even better–and it will be even more fulfilling and bring you more satisfaction than you could ever imagine. Let's get you back on track, shall we? You don't want to miss your next opportunity to fulfill your destiny. "There is no letter which cannot be used in a mantra, there is no root, which can't form some medicine, there is no person who is absolutely useless. But persons who can identify their utility and put them in proper usage are rare."- From the Sanskrit Each and every one of us is destined to find peace, purpose and passion in life during our short time here on earth. It seems quite a few of us lose sight of this purpose and slowly veer off course because we're not paying attention to our inner self. But don't worry–It is never too late to find that path that leads to your destiny in life. Never too late!

IMPORTANT–Make sure that most of your bliss from growth/ glory from action/splendor of achievement entries match with the themes of the activities you recorded for Journal exercise #1.

Some may get to the prosperous/peaceful part quicker and easier than others… but that's ok. Let's try not to hate those folks. Your day will come too. For some, your purpose will be immediately apparent, easy to accomplish for you and popular today… or at least popular in your inner circles so you'll have plenty of support from friends and family. For others, your purpose may remain a mystery for a long time, and not be extremely popular in todays' society or amongst your group of family and friends. It may take you all over the world throughout the course of your life or keep you in the same place you are now. For others it might just be a change within, and not even be apparent to your casual acquaintances. Your destiny might just be that you change into a more patient, loving, faithful, gentle, understanding person–which in-turn will make life more pleasant and might serve to provide the encouragement for someone else in your life to become the next president or the next Bill Gates and then in-turn that person donates all their money to eliminating world hunger and world peace is realized. Ok… that's stretching it a bit…. but the point is that small changes can have a profound, domino effect. You just need to seek out your path in life and the rest will fall into place. Don't compare where you are to where others appear to be. Everyone must travel their own path at their own pace. Get excited about and focus on yours.

> "You are the salt of the earth; but if the salt loses its flavor, how shall it be seasoned? The earth is then good for nothing

but to be thrown out. You are the light of the world. A city that is set on a hill cannot be hidden. Let your light so shine before men, that they may see your good works". – Matthew 5:13

It is up to every one of us to add our own individual seasoning into the stew of life. We need to spice it up with our own individual flavors. Don't think for a second that you can sneak out the kitchen and leave it up to only a few to spice up the pot. Come on now... you know that if you skimp on a recipe and put only half the number of herbs and spices that it calls for, the flavor won't be as good, and the dish will be bland. And if you had guests coming over, they wouldn't enjoy that dish and the evening wouldn't be as magical as it could be had you not held back, and served a meal with all the pizzazz and all the seasonings that the recipe called for...yeah? Well...If you are not letting your light shine at its fullest potential and not adding your full flavor to life–then it's not enough–the world will be bland and good for nothing. But sometimes we forget all the ingredients that go into a recipe. This is ok. In that case we just must refer back to the cookbook when we forget, in order to refresh our memory–right? Same goes for us as we live life... if you feel that you might be losing your flavor and going bland (if work is sucking the flava right out of ya)–then refer back to what you wrote down in the journal for exercise #1 and do something that falls in line with one of these activities to revive your Spirits and refresh your mind.

It seems like many parents try to steer their children into what they believe is the "perfect" path in life. And that this is either becoming a doctor, lawyer, accountant, or professional athlete; or either marrying a doctor, lawyer, or accountant–buying the "perfect" home and having 2.5 "perfect" children.

The thought of everyone trying to fit into this mold makes me throw up a little in my mouth. It's narrow minded, Stepford wife mentality. It's easy to follow the mainstream and do what the majority is doing. But this is like putting too much or too little seasoning into a dish... either way it won't be particularly good... yeah? It's the perfect blend of all different types of herbs and spices that make the best dishes. If everyone were confidently and happily blazing their own individual paths through life yet supporting each other along the way and enjoying the journey and growth along the way to reaching our true destinies in life, the entire world would be a better, blissful, positive place. Let me point out a few things.

At this point... No, you shouldn't trust yourself. I mean... you did get yourself into this situation. How do you know that even if you start down the "right" path now, that you won't veer off again and start living based on how someone else thinks you should live or make decisions because it's the popular one at the time or because it's what your family wants you to do or because it's best for someone else but not really the right choice for you? Maybe that idea that you have stuck in your head–that one you can't stop thinking about and imagining about how great your life will be if it works out (you know what it is); you think it's your own idea, but really, it's from an advertisement that's been playing on the radio or TV for the past few weeks or from a persuasive friend or family member that has convinced you that this is a good idea and something you should put your time, energy and money into. Marketing departments and our persuasive friends and family use an underlying formula to get us to act impulsively on their ideas. They tug at our emotional triggers of fear, guilt, envy, greed, pride, or vengeance. Once these feelings are aroused in us, we can easily be persuaded to act on impulse and thus take us off center and off our destined path. Then when the initial emotions subside you realize that it wasn't really a choice you felt totally at ease with, in the beginning but now you're stuck with the decision you made so you just compromise and stick with it for another year or so. A few actions like this and before you know it decades have gone by and you're so far from the path that you were supposed to take in life that you feel completely lost, full of regret, disappointed in yourself, trapped and worn out by life because you've spent all this time and effort trying to force something to work out for you that wasn't meant to be. Can you point out the emotional triggers in the following lines:

1. "Read this or go broke!" "You're being fattened up for the kill!" (pride)
2. Revealed Inside: The FORBIBBEN investing secret that can make you RICH! (greed)
3. What better way to show your kids how much you care! Your children will never forget this lasting gift! (guilt)
4. If you don't do this, it will just devastate your mother. She'll be so disappointed in you. Make your mother happy…come on. (guilt)
5. What… are you too chicken? Do you have to go home and ask your mommy first? (pride)

Humble yourself. Close your eyes and take several deep breaths. This time really concentrate on your breath. Close your eyes and take several breaths while placing one hand over your belly button. Hold one nostril shut while you inhale slowly for a count of five and hold the other shut while you exhale slowly for five. Listen to your breath… and imagine the path that your breath takes inside of you as you inhale deeply and exhale slowly. Imagine the path your breath travels inside.

Notice where you imagine your breath settling on the inhale and beginning from on the exhale. This is your center. Also take notice... did you get a moment of peace and quiet from all those racing thoughts in your head? This centered place is peaceful, Spiritual, and calm, with no worries. This is the place we want to be in throughout our day. We should make decisions, listen to, and respond to people from this place. You're calm, peaceful and open hearted at this moment... yeah? The next time you feel fear, anxiety, envy, pride, jealousy, or vengeance–notice that these feelings originate from a different place. These feelings resonate from doubting, fearful, envious thoughts in your head that just keep playing over and over in your mind until they produce those yucky feelings in your heart. You know the ones... "I wish I looked like that."; "I'm not smart enough or pretty enough to do this."; "How dare he treat me like that–I'll show him...etc." So what does this tell us? It tells us that all those thoughts racing through our minds–which we think are going to figure a way out of this rut and depression we're in, are in fact, the cause of our inner turmoil. They aren't from your true self/your centered/Spiritual place. They are in fact... the cause of what is draining you and driving you crazy. Following these thoughts is what caused you to veer off your destined path in the first place. In the movies when they show a person consuming a lot of alcohol, someone may say... "Oh, he's numbing the pain". Well–the guy's got a 9-to-5 and sits at a desk all day... what pain is there? It's not physical pain, his arm isn't broke, and his back isn't sore. It's mental pain and anguish, right. It's emotional pain and internal suffering that has resulted from those self-destructive thoughts resonating and running a marathon in his head. It's just those itty-bitty thoughts in our heads that stir up those bad, negative self-sabotaging feelings. And if we're not careful and don't stop those thoughts they turn into bad, negative self-sabotaging desires: destroy someone's car with a bat, shoot someone, drink a whole bottle of vodka, have promiscuous sex with guys you don't know, get some drugs. These thoughts aren't rooted in your Spiritual truth, so alcohol or drugs or another substitute is being used in this case to cope with and suffocate the incessant nagging from these thoughts that seek to destroy our soul. The thoughts that make you feel bad enough about yourself so that you will drown yourself in alcohol or turn to drugs. Maybe it's not alcohol or your traditional drugs for you... maybe it's sex for you, or a shopping addiction, or fighting with people, or gambling, or putting people down, or eating until it hurts, or pills. It happens slowly–one small compromise–giving into the desire just one time–and then just another–so that you don't recognize that you're veering off path little by little, until one day you have a moment of clarity and find yourself completely lost. And you have no idea who your true self is anymore because you've just buried your Spiritual truth so deep down.

So the goal is, to not listen to your thoughts, but to listen to your Spirit. Half of the stuff in your head is just space junk anyway. Remnants of old outdated projects and thoughts, still there, orbiting around in our heads. But we must ignore the junk and go on to do the work we're supposed to do without touching or disturbing or letting that junk hinder us. Don't bring that junk into your heart. It will just harden your heart. A considerable amount of junk stuffed in there is from the media and society; and they don't know the real you and what's best for you. Identify the options and choices you have at every point in life, and then decide to either eliminate it or act on it (I.D.E.A). Identify all options and then Decide to either Eliminate or Act upon them. And if none of the choices and options available at the time satisfies your Spirit and they don't even come close to any activities on your activities list from Exercise #1–then eliminate all options for right now and don't act on anything at the moment. Later, a new and better option will present itself. Don't operate your life based on top-down management (head to heart)–manage your life from the bottom up (heart to head). Often the trick to this is just waiting to act. You don't absolutely have to do anything right now at this time. You always have options. If you get an idea today for a new business–don't quit your job tomorrow. If a co-worker writes you an email that causes you to feel angry or annoyed–you don't have to fire back a reply right away. Draft up an email, but instead of sending the email right then, open the option menu, and choose the option to save it as a draft. Choose the draft option–then take a few deep breaths and finish out your workday. The next morning when you get to work open that draft email and read what you wrote. I bet you'll want to revise that email to make it sound less annoyed sounding and more professional and more to the point. Now–after having revised the email if you still believe the behavior needs to be addressed–send it. But now... if this colleague wants to discuss the topic further with you, you are coming from a poised, peaceful, professional standpoint (heart to head). It won't cause the collapse of civilization because you took two days to respond to an email. So slow down–we don't always have to act immediately. But boy do those infomercials tell us otherwise don't they? All of them say "act now–or you'll miss this special opportunity for additional savings. You won't be able to get this deal any place else, so you must act now!" They don't want you to take a day or two to ask friends or family what they think of the product. They don't want you to research other possibilities online or go to Walmart or the dollar store and find it for less. Society would love for us to act on impulse and buy, buy, buy... then feel guilty about it, but then grow envious of some latest gadget somebody else has... and buy, buy, buy some more. Like mindless, predictable puppets. For ideas and activities to be good and to flourish they must take root in your Spirit. And this happens from planning, research, patience, and persistence. Even those get rich quick at home opportunities will require your time and a certain skill set, quality work and persistence for you to be successful at them. But they are so good at getting you to dwell only on the thoughts and images in your head of all the lavish luxury cars you'll have within 3 months if you "act now!" It's hard to resist sometimes–but you need to wait until your heart and Spirit tells you to act. The idea needs time to get rooted in your soul before you act. And if it doesn't take root–then don't act. Here's your next journal exercise.

Journal Exercise #3: From this point on... any idea you have–whether it be to start a second job or to start taking classes in a new field or to go shopping or to remodel part of the house or to venture out and begin something like a new career that you feel you are meant to do or to move or ... anything... ANYTHING at all... write the idea down for now–don't act on any ideas just yet–just write all your ideas down in the designated pages of the journal.

This way–if you do have the next billion-dollar invention, you'll know it's safely written down, so you don't have to worry about forgetting it. Just lay it down on paper for now. Any idea... if you have an idea for an invention, if you want to purchase a fast food franchise, if you want to go to the mall to buy some new shoes, if you want to start your own restaurant, if you want to get plastic surgery, if you want to quit your job and become a fitness instructor, if you want to buy a new car or 3D TV Blu-ray player and surround sound... whatever it is. Don't do it. Just write all your ideas down for now in the journal. They are safe there. Leave plenty of space so you can come back often and elaborate on them as more thoughts come to mind on your ideas and as other new ideas come up. Prioritize the list if you'd like. Glance at it frequently. Anytime you get a few spare minutes begin to do some research on your ideas. Every few weeks/months or so read over your list of ideas and the notes you've gathered on them and elaborate on your ideas some more...reprioritize them as the ideas develop. Do a little more reading and research about your top ideas when you get the urge and jot down any beneficial information you find? For example if you get an idea for an invention one day, or if you've always wanted to open your own restaurant, or if you're thinking about starting a franchise or trying one of the numerous at home businesses that are out there or quitting your job to become a fitness instructor... these are the ideas I want you to just write down and elaborate on and research how you would go about accomplishing these ideas. As you get additional ideas or thoughts that build on these ideas you already have written down–write these down immediately too. Always keep this journal by your bedside and with you during the day, because if you're like me–your "best" ideas come to mind when you're lying in bed trying to fall asleep or in the morning in between hitting the snooze button or in the middle of a boring meeting at work. Get in the habit of writing all these ideas down as soon as you think of them. This way they are safely written down–and off your mind so they won't mentally drain you. As time goes by practice the I.D.E.A. method with these ideas. You'll notice that as time goes by... some of the ideas you have written down will loose their appeal to you. Some of the ideas may seem silly and not at all right for you after some time has passed. Or perhaps the franchise you wanted to buy is now out of business. Cross these ideas off the list, eliminate them. Could you imagine if you had quit your job and sold everything–for an idea that sounds crazy to you now? These were the ideas that never took root in your soul because they weren't in line with your Spirit/your true self and the path you are meant to travel. Thoughts in your head can always look good on the surface but your Spirit knows what's genuinely good for you.

> "The plans of the diligent lead surely to plenty, but those of everyone who is hasty, surely to poverty."–Proverbs 21:5

So, I bet you're thinking to yourself.... "This is easier said than done." Sure–you can see the benefit of taking your time and figuring out all the options available to you before making decisions and that being in a peaceful/centered state all the time is ideal–and you might be reading this on one of those rare occasions when you're relaxed and don't have a million things on your to do list or a house full of kids that all have the flu. But I bet your experience tells you that this Zen moment only lasts for a moment and then you'll get up Monday morning and it's off to the races... and you're back in the middle of the fast-paced, go-go-go, need a decision now world that we live in, with the endless errands, 24/7 work schedules, endless bills, dropping the kids off, picking the kids up, dealing with all the unexpected problems and emergencies that come up during the day, trying to make time to spend with friends and keep up with facebook... etc. From the time you get up in the morning until the time you go to bed, you're moving at breakneck speed just skimming the surface, you're thinking to yourself... I don't have time to pause for deep introspective, reflective, Spiritual moments during the day. So, when it comes to making a life altering/path changing decision at the end of a long soul-grinding day, you're moving so fast or you're numb from trying to get as much done as you can in one day, that you end up acting on the first thought that pops into your head on an issue without taking a "gut check".

This has got to be scary now that we've established those ideas and thoughts in our heads aren't all that reliable. All day long ideas and impressions about people places and things are being crammed into our head by society stereotypes from media, friends, family, co-workers, and advertisers that subtly mold how we think about certain topics. They are constantly pushing and pulling on you from all angels until they push you to act and you choose to do what they want you to do, before you've even had time to pause for a deep breath to center yourself and identify all the options that are available to you, and to make sure you're confident that your Spirit is ok with the decision before you make it. "A gut check"–I believe I've heard it called. The purpose of this book and journaling exercises are to help you to build a strong Spiritual foundation that will help launch you onto the right path that will lead you to your destiny in life and keep you from veering off course again. And this… is what will fill you with the joy, contentment, and inner peace that you desire. My goal is to help get you to a point where you will easily live and make decisions in your life from that centered, Spiritual place all the time–no matter how hectic and volatile the environment is around you, and to get you in-tune with your true self and recognizing your soul's desires. But you'll need to get connected to your Spirit first. This is the key step. You must connect or re-connect to your Spirit. Getting connected to and following your Spirits' desire will help you eliminate regret, thus eliminate guilt, thus you will start to feel pleased and satisfied with yourself–thus happy and content about your life and the way that it is progressing. This is going to take research, patience, and persistence but we can do it.

We've already established that we haven't done such a great job maneuvering through life on our own. So give this a try. The alternative, of just continuing along in life with your same old routine and letting the world shove you around and knock you down and drag you into whatever box it wants to stuff you in… doesn't sound so great either. So, what do you say… give this book and these journal exercises a try?

Here's a scenario for you: Say after a horrible night's sleep and a long, busy, exceptionally stressful day, where you felt like you were being attacked for every idea you presented at work and cut off, every time you tried to make a comment, and to top it all off you had a poor performance review and didn't get a raise this year. You're on your way home from work still fuming from all the things that went wrong that day, wishing they would fire all the people that got on your nerves and daydreaming about leaving for lunch one day or taking all your vacation days and never coming back… when just then an ad comes on the radio for a special at your favorite pizza place–a buy one large pizza get a second one free. And then the radio announces a one day sale at MACY's–everything is 50% off. And then there is an ad for $2 margaritas at your favorite local bar. And then…an infomercial comes on the air announcing a new breakthrough at home business that is guaranteed to make you $100,000 a week if you just follow their step-by-step no fail plan. You'll be able to quit your job by the end of the month and travel the world and pay off all your bills. You start thinking to yourself… "After the day I just had, I deserve to pig out till it hurts and shop 'til I drop and have a couple margaritas." After all, … you're guaranteed to become a millionaire within a year. You call and order the CD program for the at home business and then head straight for the margaritas. After happy hour you're off to the Mall, excited about all the great deals you're going to find. Now back in your car after shopping you're thinking to yourself that you shouldn't have bought so much but you just couldn't decide which outfit to put back, so you took that as a sign that you were supposed to keep everything. You call and order two large pizzas and stop and get a movie on the way home. You can't wait to get home and sink down into your couch and tear up that pizza and end the night with a good movie.. ... The next morning you wake up with a major case of heart burn and regret, wishing you hadn't eaten so much...you'd been doing so well... now your 3 lbs. heavier. And then you add up the receipts from everything you spent last night and look to see what you can take back–but you've taken the tags off everything already. Yesterday you were full of vengeance and anger at your job and co-workers for not treating you better and today you're angry at yourself. A few days go by and the at home business CD you ordered shows up on your doorstep. Turns out it was a big scam–there was nothing on it you can use. Now you're stuck feeling frustrated, down on yourself and trapped in this life, with a job you don't like. Stuck in this endless loop you can't seem to get out of. Things start to look up for a few weeks...and then the scenario just repeats itself. And all you are achieving is that you're becoming more and more depressed, more and more in debt and weighing more and more...Errrrrrr. Think back to when you've had a bad day. When your emotions were running high–from when you've had a horrible night's sleep, your frustrated and irritable, and it seemed like no one was listening to you and that everyone was against you and nothing was going your way. And you couldn't stop thinking about how you wanted to just show everyone just how good you are and to put them in their place for once so they would give you the respect you desire. Advertisements online, and on the radio, TV, and in magazines feed into these thoughts of envy, fear, pride, vengeance, jealousy, lust... and they can trick you into thinking that you need to buy some "thing", and that you need it now, to give you the satisfaction and the happiness in life that you so deserve... especially after the day you've just had. Your emotions are running hot and those destructive thoughts swirling around in your head slowly seep down into your heart; you're unaware of their subtle covert attacks. Their mission is to create feelings that will produce an overwhelming desire that you need it...that you need this "thing". And as the thoughts get more and more and more focused and louder and louder and louder the desire gets more and more intense–until you act, and buy-buy-buy, or indulge-indulge-indulge or binge-binge-binge. Telling yourself that you deserve it after the day you've had–oh yeah... that's what will make you feel better. Pssst!........ it's a lie! Then what happens... the movie is over, and you've realized just how many "bad fat" calories you've consumed when you weren't even all that hungry to begin with. Or you get up the next morning and realize you have similar clothes like the items you've just bought, and you've already ripped off the tags so you can't return anything, or you've woken up to a throbbing headache after drinking way more then you had intended to and you can't even remember the whole evening. Yesterday you were upset with other people for not treating you right–but you have no control over other people. Now... you're upset with yourself–and you do have control over your actions. You feel guilt and regret for the fact that you let your emotions get the best of you. You don't deserve that! This causes you to not feel good about yourself. So now to overcompensate you set this hard goal for yourself–like to start this intense exercise and diet program at the gym after work that begins tomorrow but then... that doesn't happen...so now you're feeling even worse about yourself. This is tearing your emotional wellbeing and self-esteem down little by little making it easier for you to give in to the temptation the next time around. Then what happens... maybe you're out one day and someone is slightly rude to you unintentionally and you go crazy and let 'em have it–cursing at the person and almost going to blows...calling them all kinds of names...when really you're just projecting your own self-hate and frustrations on other people. So, it's looking like you're not even really in control of yourself. Just like your immune system is more susceptible to diseases if weakened–if your emotional system and wellbeing is weakened or comprised then you're going to be more susceptible to giving into self-destructive tempting thoughts and doing what the media and society tells you to do and not following your own path and being true to yourself. And if these negative behaviors become a habit and a part of your life more and more it can lead to a downward spiral that leads straight to rock bottom. Most of us start out with a strong emotional system that's built up by loving parents, family, and friends before we're left on our own to face the evil world and the forces that try to tear us down. But then there are some people that never had their emotional systems built up at all as children. However, they still must go out there and face the evil world just like everybody else. My heart aches for people who grow up in extremely poor countries that have lost their parents to war or human rights atrocities or people who grow up in drug infested abusive homes. Their emotional well-being may not be strong... thus like a weak immune system, these children and eventually adults may be more susceptible to self-destructive thoughts seeping into their soul and desiring to engage in self destructive behaviors. Imagine if this was the person you projected all your self hate onto. They don't deserve that. Don't make matters worse. But here's the thing... even if this is the situation... if you come from abuse are in it now or are leading a lifestyle that's headed straight for it...there is a Spirit on the inside of each and every one of us that isn't affected by the outside world and all of its evil and negativity, it's always there, fully intact. The difference is we're either not connect to it, aren't even aware of it, or are only partially connected. It's just buried deep down. I want you to be fully connected. There are many beliefs that are so engrained in mainstream society and within our sub-cultures that actually hinder and don't help us in life, but we don't even think about it. We just believe some things without question. You're in college–you're supposed to be a party girl or be the guy that can drink anyone under the table. Or our personal prejudices about either other races or particular places and things that we just believe because it's what our parents told us growing up, but we've never actually thought about for ourselves. These are the types of things I want you to question and test. Pause and really think about where your unquestioned beliefs come from. You've got to take inventory of all your thoughts and beliefs and test everything to make sure it's not a bad habit and a stumbling block in your life or a belief that just isn't right. Let's not just blindly follow. Think about whether a particular thought or behavior pattern may be leading you down a wrong path in life. It's almost like our enemy has set these thoughts and beliefs into our society to cast a wide net. Most of us will leave the bar when happy hour is over if we have school or a test or big presentation the next day ... but the ones that don't, get caught in the net. The net of lies. And if you don't think media and the advertisements you listen to or watch every day over the years has an impact on your behavior and choices then read this statistic. Roughly 70 percent of blacks smoke menthols, compared with just over 20 percent of whites and 26 percent of Hispanics, according to the latest government data. Health.com: 70 years of menthol cigarette ads "Menthol cigarettes are marketed to the most vulnerable sectors of our society, particularly starting in the 1960s," Gardiner says. "It's essentially predatory marketing."[1] Since way back menthol cigarette companies have been strategically advertising to blacks and guess who smokes the most menthol... So if you're constantly thinking negative thoughts and giving into self-destructive desires and the pressure to follow a path and direction in life that goes against your true Spirit–guess who'll miss their destiny. Imagine instead... that even though you felt those self-destructive thoughts and desires on your drive home from work after an especially grueling, emotionally draining day–you waited to act, drove straight home and took a few of those deep breaths we did earlier, immediately turned on the radio and danced around in the family room, did a 20 minute exercise routine, spent 15 minutes stretching, then read an interesting article, or researched an exotic healthy recipe and then went to the store to pick up the ingredients for your culinary experiment...something from your activities list we created in Journal Exercise #1, or sat and thought about what it is you could do for Journal Exercise #2 and do that. Before you know it... a couple of hours have gone by and you haven't even thought about work or whatever it was that had you all twisted up and frustrated earlier. And you feel good about yourself because your Spirit is in control and empowered, not those destructive evil thoughts. This is like a save point for your soul.

---

[1] http://www.cnn.com/2010/HEALTH/06/15/menthol.cigarettes/index.html?hpt=C2

If deleterious transactions have happened to your Spirit; If you've gotten off track slightly and you feel like you've lost yourself a little, you'll want to find what it is that can be your save point to rollback to. An activity that you know refreshes your mind and re-centers your Spirit before continuing along on your path. If you've had a crappy day and you're feeling lousy, what is it for you that will re-center you and get you back to living heart to head, because you don't want the wrong thoughts contaminating your heart. And then, if you were to go out to dinner or still felt like watching a movie or going to the mall you are more likely to consume a healthy portion of food or if you see an awesome outfit at the mall it will be easier for you to walk away if it's not in the budget. No rush. I'm not saying that none of these work-from-home opportunities are legitimate–but wouldn't you feel better about yourself and your decision if you asked other people if they have tried anything similar, and did research into the company and similar companies like it and really understood the amount of time you will have to dedicate to it to make the money they are claiming you can make. Everything takes time and effort to produce good positive long-lasting results. Everything! After you've done some research and sat on the idea for a while and planned out when would be the best time to start... that's if the idea doesn't get eliminated from your list... at least then, if it doesn't work out, you shouldn't feel regret because you honesty did what you felt was right for you. No shame in that. Maybe you weren't supposed to be successful at it because it was supposed to teach you a lesson that you will need for an even better opportunity that will be coming along later in your life on the journey to your destiny.

"Pride goes before destruction, and a haughty Spirit before a fall. Better to be of a humble Spirit with the lowly, than to divide the spoil with the proud."- Proverbs 16:18

Society pressures us to "keep moving forward", like something is wrong with us if we're not money hungry and our goal isn't to climb the corporate ladder as fast as possible and if we don't aspire to have an eight-bedroom mansion and a Mercedes and get married and then have 2.5 kids by the time we're thirty. Society tells us that we must keep "moving up" and that we are not successful in life if we don't go from an apartment to a town home to a single family home to a bigger house… and from an entry level position to a senior position to a manager to a director to vice president to CEO… from no car to a Subaru to a Mercedes to a Bentley…and unless we're married…and unless we have all the latest electronic gadgets and entertainment systems. These are beliefs subtly weaved into the fabric of society. And it was done so well and so smoothly that we didn't even know our thoughts and beliefs about what is most important were changing, ever so slightly into believing that this is what we are supposed to aspire to in life and what will make us happy and that this should be our focus and goal in life. It's subtle but the pressure is there; more for some. And because this message is self-serving and superficial and doesn't come from anything that resonates with our Spirit we end up with a culture in society that doesn't have time for family, that is full of criticism, that doesn't put others first and doesn't stop to help others who may have stumbled and lost their way. These thoughts and beliefs contaminate and harden the heart… burying the Spirit within us. If all that matters is having money and a Bentley and that this is what will make me happy then I'll just take someone else's. That's a quick and easy way to success and happiness. It may just be my impression—but it seems like back in the day—what was more important than anything was being a person with integrity and good character and seeking a good name within your church community. Helping people out when we could and looking out for each other and taking the time to get to know your neighbors. Remember Matthew 3:15? If everyone were to follow the same path in life then the world will be bland and good for nothing. Are we becoming good for nothing because we're all just following a path we were told to follow or think we're supposed to follow in life and not thinking for ourselves—thus not utilizing our own individual talents? Which is resulting in a society that is losing joy and happiness, thus resulting in more crime and dysfunction? This makes me think of that movie, "The Pursuit of Happiness", when the wife of Will Smiths' character, played by Thandie Newton thought that going from an unsuccessful salesman to an unpaid intern at a Wall Street firm was going backwards in life. This frustrated her to the point that she left him. She believed the lies of society… that a successful person is someone who keeps making more and more money every year, and someone that never fails at anything or makes a mistake on anything and that if you live in an apartment you "need to" move to a townhouse and then a single family home—and that these things are the measure of how well your family is doing and how content you are in life. Going from working 1 shift to 3 at McDonalds, will bring in more money—yes, but if you didn't work at all for a short time while going to college to earn a degree or certificate that would result in a career that paid twice as much as McDonalds, while working half the hours—then no job and no income for the short term would be better in the long run. Linda, the wife in that movie never paused long enough to take several deep breaths, do a "gut check", analyze all ideas with her husband, or research the opportunity her boyfriend Chris was trying to pursue. She was probably so consumed with pride and fearful thoughts racing through her head day-in and day-out during this time in her life that she was probably a slave to these thoughts, consuming her mind every second of the day eventually hardening her heart. The thoughts running through her head probably said that she was dumb for believing in her boyfriend's bone density machines and that he's not going to amount to anything, so she'd be even more stupid to trust him now with this new idea. She probably never got a moment's relief from those negative, destructive, doubting thoughts and the pressures from society probably got to be too much for her and out of desperation to do something to relieve the pressure and to make it better she acted on the first thought that came to mind... to leave. She probably couldn't bear the thought of the humiliation and hardship and hurt pride that she would endure if she were to have put her faith and had stuck by her man's internship idea and it failed just like the salesman gig had and they were all living on the street. What if Will Smiths character, Chris Gardner, had given into the pressures also and given up on that idea and just went out and got one or two or three minimum wage jobs just to better their financial situation as quick as possible and to please his wife to make her feel like they were "moving up" in the world because they could buy more groceries this week or get an extra cable channel. He would have worked himself into the ground, never realizing his amazing destiny that awaited him. He would've been consumed by regret and "what ifs", had he not followed his Spirit and gone after that internship. He would've felt lost and trapped in an unfulfilling life in this land of opportunity and worn out every day from thinking what if I had tried for that internship ... would I have gotten the position.

Instead–he listened to and followed his Spirit's desire to reach for the stars and as a result no regrets–bliss, glory, splendor, and happiness were his at last. But what did I tell you... it took research, patience and persistence. Perhaps his girlfriend leaving him was all part of his journey to reaching his destiny. Maybe he wouldn't have been as persistent and driven to win if his girlfriend had stayed. Who knows? But In a movie the characters life story is condensed down to 2 short hours, so we can clearly see immediately how every decision effect the characters life and mind-set either negatively or positively and that some setbacks and hardships actually end up helping the character to reach their destiny and achieve the happy ending they were seeking and then they realize that it was all worth it in the end. It is clean cut and clearly laid out for us in a movie. But in real life it takes longer to get to the end, and it is so hard to know which choices we're supposed to make that will help shape us and lead us down the path to our destiny. If the choice, we make–makes life harder and more uncomfortable for us– how do we know when to throw in the towel or when not to? In a movie the audience roots for the character to not give up, and to hang in there, because we usually know the story line ahead of time. We know without a doubt that the movie will end on a successful, happy note for the character. So, the audience doesn't feel fear, or isn't critical of the character when he/she makes mistakes. Instead, we're encouraging. Put yourself in the "real life" Chris Gardner's shoes for a minute and imagine the doubt and fear that must have kept trying to pollute his heart and the inner strength he must have had to persevere. I can only imagine the type of doubts that would've plagued my mind: "What am I thinking... I'm not good enough to get this position. What is everyone going to think of me if I fall short again? They are going to laugh at me and tell me I was stupid for even trying.

I'm such a looser. I can't even provide my son his own bed to sleep in and a hot home cooked meal. I never thought I'd be homeless. Maybe I should've given my son up. Maybe I should quit going after this Wall Street internship and just take any job–shining shoes and get on welfare." Week after week in a homeless shelter... pursuing an idea that you only "think" might work to bring you and your family security and happiness. How many weeks could you have lasted? I probably would've gone crazy and given up at that point in the movie when Chris gave his instructor his last five dollars, or when he had to pick up his dry cleaning. I probably would've given it to him right there and spewed out all my frustrations on him right there and said, "You ain't punkin me... I quit". Or cried and said life's not fair... why me... I quit? When life isn't fun anymore and it gets tough and the work gets hard we tend to get weary and to lose hope and lose patience–we begin to veer off course and eventually just give up on whatever it is we were going after whether it's losing weight or pursuing a degree while still working fulltime and raising a family or writing a book or becoming a singer or actor. We give up and settle for where we are in life, the status quo, never dreaming big dreams again or believing that we could ever accomplish something great...when we might have been just one decision or only one week away from a breakthrough and reaching our destiny had we just hung in there and persevered and humbled ourselves even more and hung in there just a little while longer. But it gets so frustrating in real life when we don't know how much exactly "a little while longer" is. Don't you wish you had a personal guide through life that you could trust in completely? Or an instruction manual that would tell you what to do and what not to do in every situation in life?

A New You

Well, I've got Good News for you… It turns out there is a guide and an instruction manual for life that we can believe in and trust with our whole heart to lead us down the right path in life. Unfortunately, though–the fight between good and evil is very much alive in this world. And the evil one doesn't want you to know that this guide and instruction manual for life exists. The evil one has done a good job up to this point of slowly weaving his lies deep into the belief and thought system of main-stream society. So much so, that a lot of people have no clue that some of their firmly held beliefs and thought patterns are based on lies and that their conscious is numb to the point of not even thinking to question why it is we think a particular way about something, and if it's the right way that God would like us to think. The evil one wants us to wander around through life with no real purpose, trying to "find ourselves". He also loves it if we start doing really well at what we pursue and get really busy in life and really focused on work, money, social activities, school, cars…etc., and feel so proud of ourselves for all that we've accomplished on our own and that we're better than others because the world is at our fingertips due to wealth, popularity or prestige and for us to think that we've got everything under control–nothing can touch us. He also loves it if we hit a stumbling block and our world comes tumbling down. The money dries up, the fame disappears, no more accolades, our health deteriorates, we hit rock bottom and lose it all. He would love for you to over work trying to get more money… or over work trying to please people. He would love for you to think that you don't have time to go to church or read the Bible or to even think about God. The evil world wants us to be superficial, in-secure, angry, worn down, defeated. This makes us easier to manipulate. We'll be more likely to fall for its lies; hook line and sinker, and less likely to question the status quo or seek to find the truth in everything. And less likely to speak up and get in the way when the system is wrong. And so, you'll think you're limited based on the worlds' criteria and options. The evil one wants the world to become good for nothing. But… When Jesus left this world, he sent the Spirit of God, the Holy Spirit, as a gift to be our guide and our helper throughout life, to help steer us and to keep us on course along a path toward our God given destiny in life. The Bible is our instruction manual for life and through its words God speaks directly to the Holy Spirit that is within us. And that Spirit then fills our heart with the love and wisdom and truth of our Creator. This is the heart that we want influencing the thoughts in our mind (heart to head). Our first goal is to establish a connection with and then strengthen that connection to the Spirit, so that we can continually grow in the knowledge and wisdom and love of Jesus. So what do you think…? It makes sense, yeah? Think about this…

> "That which is born of the flesh is flesh, and that which is born of the Spirit is Spirit. Do not marvel that I said to you, 'You must be born again.' The wind blows where it wishes, and you hear it, but cannot tell where it comes from and where it goes. So is everyone who is born of the Spirit." – John 3: 6-8

We're born of the flesh, so satisfying our fleshly desires comes easily for us. I think I read somewhere that children as young as two begin lying and manipulating, trying to get their way. It comes natural for us. But to then realize that there is another level... a Spiritual part within us that has desires as well... this doesn't come as easily at first because it goes against our fleshly desires. Especially for those of us that didn't grow up in an environment where the Spirit was recognized or if there was a lack of structure and discipline. It's like swimming upstream; like walking against the crowd. It can be tough to fight against your fleshly desires and get to the point where you have formed a connection to and are growing in that connection with the Holy Spirit. But when you do–and are "born again in the Spirit", you'll be able to recognize the Holy Spirits' presence in your life like the blowing wind. You can't see it–but you will feel it and hear it and you can tell when it's around you. The evil one has done a good job of keeping this truth out of mainstream society. You agree? He doesn't want us to connect with the Holy Spirit inside of us that was our gift from God, nor trust in the Bible that God has given to us as our instruction manual. Because then we will know our true selves and our full potential and let our light shine, and he wants us to be all about the flesh and be limited to what the world says we can do and not what God says we can do. It's like if your parents gave a letter and a gift to your friend to give to you at school that will help you when studying for finals–and your "friend" gives you the letter minus the gift. After some time goes by you realize that that "friend" lied to you intentionally putting a stumbling block in your way by not giving you the gift. And all this time you've probably done a lot of things just because your friend said so, and now you're wondering what else she has lied to you about or manipulated you into doing. Yes–I believe the evil one has done a good job at hiding the fact that the gift of the Holy Spirit exists, and he's manipulated the culture and belief/thought structure of our society into believing that the Bible is not relevant in our lives today and that we don't need to be connected to God through Jesus, and that we don't need to spend time with Him to have successful, good, genuinely happy lives. And that we don't need His protection as a trusting, true friend and perfect, protective loving Father. Jesus and the Bible was never spoken of in this way in my home growing up, nor at friends' homes when I was visiting, nor in school.... not even in the church I went to (well... it probably was–I just wasn't paying attention then). I thought a Bible was like a diploma. That it was just supposed to sit on the shelf, collecting dust and looking antique. I never gave it a moment's thought. I thought it was good enough just to say, "Yeah I believe in God…yeah–yeah–yeah, I believe Jesus is going to come back one day to judge the living and the dead." And that's where my thoughts ended on the subject. Not very deep. I assumed I could create my best life and build my best destiny on my own without any help, and that it would only be on my dying bed when I would see the light–and only then would it matter whether one acknowledges Jesus or not. He would run through my entire life right then and there and if the good outweighed the bad, he would reach down and give me a hand into heaven. I never thought…what if at that point he says… "Who are you? Do I know you?" "I don't recall you ever speaking to Me?" "I never heard a prayer from you." I mean talk about embarrassing… could you imagine… standing in line at the pearly gates and getting denied access. I don't know about ya'll ... but I'd rather get denied at La Perla Night club for not being "cool" enough, then get denied at "the" pearly gates. I want to spend time getting to know Jesus now to make sure I get on the guest list when the time comes... know what I'm saying?

An eye for an eye. How many of us grew up with that mantra? Have you ever thought about it deeper and researched it? Have you wondered if it's correct? If it is a belief we want to continue circulating in our society? If someone punched someone in the arm in high school, you best believe he was going to get punched right back. And some people believe that if someone takes a life, he/she deserves to have their life taken as penalty. But is this just because people will call us sissies or soft if we don't retaliate with a show of vengeance and strength, so do we only say we believe in "An eye for an eye" just to appear tough and to please others? What about this one... is your excuse for not reading the Bible because the Bible is written in old English or some sort of Shakespeare type language and it's hard to read and those people back in that era couldn't have possibly written anything that could help or be relevant to you today anyway. Have you questioned where that thought came from in your head? Why do you think that? Read these passages that are directly from the New King James version of the Holy Bible that you can pick up at any Christian bookstore and then tell me if this could have been about our current times if I hadn't told you it came from the Bible.

> "Flee also youthful lusts; but pursue righteousness, faith, love, peace with those who call on the Lord out of a pure heart. But avoid foolish and ignorant disputes, knowing that they generate strife. And a servant of the Lord must not quarrel but be gentle to all, able to teach, patient, in humility correcting those who are in opposition, if God perhaps will grant them repentance, so that they may know the truth, and that they may come to their senses and escape

the snare of the devil, having been taken captive by him to do his will. But know this, that in the last days perilous times will come: For men will be lovers of themselves, lovers of money, boasters, proud, blasphemers, disobedient to parents, unthankful, unholy, unloving, unforgiving, slanderers, without self-control, brutal, despisers of good, traitors, headstrong, haughty, lovers of pleasure rather than lovers of God, having a form of godliness but denying its power. And from such people turn away! For of this sort are those who creep into households and make captives of gullible women loaded down with sins, led away by various lusts, always learning and never able to come to the knowledge of the truth. Now as Jannes and Jambres resisted Moses, so do these also resist the truth: men of corrupt minds, disapproved concerning the faith; but they will progress no further, for their folly will be manifest to all, as theirs also was. But you have carefully followed my doctrine, manner of life, purpose, faith, patience, love, perseverance, persecutions, afflictions, which happened to me at Antioch, at Iconium, at Lystra – what persecutions I endured. And out of them all, the Lord delivered me. Yes, and all who desire to live godly in Christ Jesus will suffer persecution. But evil men and impostors will grow worse and worse, deceiving and being deceived. But you must continue in the things which you have learned and been assured of, knowing from whom you have learned them, and that from childhood you have known the Holy Scriptures, which are able to make you wise for salvation through faith which is in Christ Jesus. All Scripture is given by inspiration of God, and is profitable for doctrine, for reproof, for correction, for instruction in righteousness, that the man of God may be complete, thoroughly equipped for every good work."–Timothy 2: 22-26, 3:1-17

When we're young we tend to be foolish and we have lusts and desires that can distract us and lead us down the wrong path in life and attempt to draw us into a lifestyle by fooling us into thinking it's fun and fabulous and the best life anyone could hope for–but often this life leads to a life full of regret and unfulfilled potential. During this foolish time in our lives, it is often the time when arguments and disputes can get out of hand and lead to bad accidents happening over stupid stuff. Recently I heard on the news of a young girl that died after being jumped by a group of other girls just because she talked to a boy one of the other girls liked. In some high school communities' kids got robbed if they're wearing a popular pair of shoes or the latest fashionable jacket and then this led to retaliation and innocent people got shot or injured in the process. If someone is "disrespected" by someone in another crew, the next day both neighborhoods are in the parking lot after school to fight it out. And all of it could've been over something as small as being gritted on in the hallway. I think about these types of actions and way of thinking and think to myself, "how dumb". How dumb are we adults–that we let these corrosive patterns of behavior and beliefs creep into the culture of our society without speaking out when the scriptures have been here this whole time to instruct us in what's right and what to say. When we get older, we tend to pursue peace more with others–but it's not necessarily because we've seen the error of our youthful ways and have found the Spirit… it's more likely just because I can't afford to miss work or show up to work with a black eye or busted lip and I'm too tired and emotionally drained after work to even care about arguing with someone. I just want to eat, watch some TV, and then go to bed. But the real reason that we should flee from evil, foolish ways is because we've discovered the truth in the Scriptures, and we are seeking to follow and please the Spirit and not people. And this truth, is what should be talked about and explained to our children in our homes and in our friend's homes while our children are visiting and in school–so they don't get caught in the snare of the devil and begin to believe that the foolish way of life or thug mentality is the right way to live. Those 24 year old guys that still hang out in high school parking lots and come up to school to fight high school kids and flirt with 15 year old girls... those guys are an example of caught in the snare. This pleases the enemy doesn't it? This is how he builds his army to do his work of burying the truth deeper and deeper trying to keep us further and further from our Father, until we are so consumed by that which is ignorant and foolish and unimportant that we can't recognize the truth when we hear it, and the concepts of righteousness, faith, love, peace, and a pure heart are foreign to us. But this example is a no brainer. No one would disagree that when we're young we act and think foolishly and are not always good. But what about right now? Have you ever stopped to think if there was any behavior or current thought pattern in your current way of life that might also be foolish and be serving the devil and not God? I mean... when we're young and in the middle of it, we don't think that we're acting foolishly–we just think it's old people/parents trying to keep us from having fun. It's not until we look back, that we realize that we were stupid for thinking and doing some of the things we thought and did. So, is it possible then that right now there is something you think that is foolish and only when you look back on your whole life will you realize it? Actually...I'm sure, that there is something we all currently believe that's foolish.

We're not perfect. Does nothing come to mind...? Then this is a bad sign. There must be a tremendous number of things because society seems to be leaning more towards the perilous times described above: putting ourselves first, lovers of money, boasters, proud, disobedient to parents, unthankful, unholy, unloving, unforgiving, slanderers, without self-control, brutal, despisers of good, traitors, headstrong, haughty, lovers of pleasure rather than lovers of God. I don't know about you, but I think these Bible verses are easy to understand and are astonishingly relevant to the times we live in now. So now that we are open to the idea that parts of our mentality and belief system up to this point might be influenced by the devil–what can be done about it? What is the antidote? The answer is in this passage of Timothy you just read above. In the Holy Scriptures, which can make you wise for salvation through faith which is in Christ Jesus. Follow my doctrine, manner of life, purpose, faith, patience, love, perseverance, persecutions, afflictions. Yes, and all who desire to live godly in Christ Jesus will suffer persecution. But out of them all, the Lord will deliver you. But evil men and impostors will grow worse and worse, deceiving and being deceived. But you must continue in the things which you have learned and been assured of, knowing from whom you have learned them. There's going to be persecutions and hardships in life regardless. So, the question you must ask yourself is would you rather be persecuted for foolishness like sticking up for a friend who wants to go jump a guy for talking to his girl or would you rather be persecuted for trying to live like the one and only Jesus Christ and ensuring your salvation. All Scripture is given by inspiration of God and is profitable for doctrine (for teaching as a belief system), for criticism, for correction, for instruction in righteousness, that the man of God may be complete, thoroughly equipped for every good work."

If you are not connected to–and cannot feel the Holy Spirit working in you and in your life, then you're going to have a harder time maneuvering through the twists and turns and ups and downs and heartaches that life will bring you down here in the "real world". As I think we've experienced already–right? And it doesn't matter who you are. You could have a $trillion dollars in the bank and live in a mansion with a butler and a driver... it's still going to be a bumpy ride.

It's not what you know, it's who you know. This is another popular saying/belief in our society, right? So, who would you rather know... the senator of your state–that may be able to pull a few favors for you to get your child into a prestigious school or upgrade your seat at a state function? But if a sex scandal comes out surrounding that senator are you going to want to be associated with him then? Or be seen sitting next to him then? Or have your child and family connected to him then? Human beings are human beings–born of the flesh. We cannot be guaranteed or certified to never screw up. Or would you rather know your Creator and the Creator of the universe and be friends with his only Son who can put in a good word for you with the Big Guy upstairs? Say for instance, you're over at a friend's house and that friend tells you that another friend you two have in common is getting divorced from her husband and that he cheated on her and all sorts of other juicy gossip. The first thing you're going to do when you get home is call your friend to find out if it's true, right. You're going to want to hear it directly from the source and get the full story–right? Well... the next time someone or society tries to tell you what they think you should do with your life or you're having a hard time deciding about something... or you've made up your mind to do something already... or you want to verify how you should think or act in a certain situation...anything. Find some alone time, open the Bible, and begin to read the Scriptures. Before and while you're reading, ask God to speak to your heart and to open your eyes to the truth and to the direction you should go in life. Get the whole truth directly from the source. If you've lost your way, if you feel like you're on the wrong path in life and you're wondering which way to go–or if you're looking to be the best, complete person you can be; then the Bible/Holy Scriptures is your source for correcting you and getting you back on track and keeping you on track with instructions on the manner in which you shall live that will make you wise. Don't think that you're going to just open the Bible first thing to a random page and BOOM!, the first words you read are going to be the answer to your specific question. And then you close the Bible and never open it again until the next time you have another question…and then BOOM! Don't let the evil world ruin this for you. While you're practicing patience and perseverance, the evil one is going to try and talk you out of it. The evil one doesn't want you to take the time to get beneath the surface and to ponder the true meaning of words spoken in society and in the media, to seek out the truth in the Scriptures and find it. From the worlds perspective there is no time for all that in this fast-paced go-go-go, individualistic society we live in. If it looks good and sounds good to you then go with it–don't ask questions–no need to verify. There may be a time when the first few words you read after picking up the Bible may be the answer to a question you have, however–you may not realize it at the time you're reading it. But after some time passes… like say a month later, you'll be driving down the road and suddenly… it hits you like a ton of bricks… Ah Ha! Now I get it!! Now–after growing some in wisdom during the month that passed you understand what it was that you read in the Bible a month ago and now you realize how you can apply it to your life today. This is bliss from growth. Write this down in your journal when it happens. And then you're going to feel all guilty for not trusting that God would show you the answer, because it didn't happen on your time and in the way you wanted. But we don't always know best. We withhold information from our children if we feel like they are too young to fully understand. Well… we are all children to God, and he does the same for us as we grow in wisdom from the Scriptures. God created the world and everything in it. You are his creation. Say it several times…go ahead, say it out load… "I am Gods creation." And he didn't leave you out here all by yourself. He gave you an owner's manual and a means to communicate with him.

> "These things I have spoken to you, that you should not be made to stumble. They will put you out of the synagogues; yes, the time is coming that who-ever kills you will think that he offers God service. And these things they will do to you because they have not known the Father nor Me. But these things I have told you, that when the time comes, you may remember that I told you of them. And these

things I did not say to you at the beginning, because I was with you. But now I go away to Him who sent Me, and none of you asks Me, 'Where are You going?' But because I have said these things to you, sorrow has filled your heart. Nevertheless, I tell you the truth. It is to your advantage that I go away; for if I do not go away, the Helper will not come to you; but if I depart, I will send Him to you. And when He has come, He will convict the world of sin, and of righteousness, and of judgment: of sin, because they do not believe in Me; of righteousness, because I go to My Father and you see Me no more; of judgment, because the ruler of this world is judged. I still have many things to say to you, but you cannot bear them now. However, when He, the Spirit of truth, has come, He will guide you into all truth; for He will not speak on His own authority, but whatever He hears He will speak; and He will tell you things to come. He will glorify Me, for He will take of what is Mine and declare it to you. All things that the Father has are Mine. Therefore, I said that He will take of Mine and declare it to you.–John 16: 1-15

When you go to stay at a hotel or go to an amusement park or stay in someone else's home don't you get a guided tour by the owner or pick up a map, so you know where everything is, and what time all the shows start. This is so you know what is going on, so that you don't miss out on anything good and to help you maneuver around the place easier while you're there, which makes your stay more pleasant. Imagine if you didn't get a map or get a tour. You would just wander around with no purpose, no direction–just hoping to get lucky and stumble upon the entrance to a cool new ride. You'd probably stumble a few times… run into a few dead ends… be in one place when really you should be in another. You wouldn't have as pleasant a time. Well… the same goes for your life while you're in this world. God has a wonderful plan for our lives and things he wants us to do for our benefit and to glorify him. But we miss out on these wonderful things and our best life possible and have a less then pleasant stay if we don't allow ourselves to get the guided tour: pray and listen to the Holy Spirit and refer to the map often- the Bible.

> "To You, O Lord, I lift up my soul. O my God, I trust in You; Let me not be ashamed; Let not my enemies' triumph over me. Indeed, let no one who waits on You be ashamed; Let those be ashamed who deal treacherously without cause. Show me Your ways, O LORD; Teach me Your paths. Lead me in Your truth and teach me, For You are the God of my salvation; On You I wait all the day. Remember, O LORD, Your tender mercies and Your loving kindnesses, For they are from of old. Do not remember the sins of my youth, nor my transgressions; According to Your mercy remember me, For Your goodness' sake, O LORD. Good and upright is the LORD; Therefore He teaches sinners in the way. The humble He guides in justice, And the humble He teaches His way. All the paths of the LORD are mercy and truth, To such as keep His covenant and His testimonies. For Your name's sake, O LORD, Pardon my iniquity, for it is great. Who is the man that fears the LORD? Him shall He teach in the way He chooses. He himself shall dwell in prosperity, And his descendants shall inherit the earth. The secret of the LORD is with those who fear Him, And He will show them His covenant, My eyes are ever toward the LORD, For He shall pluck my feet out of the net. Turn Yourself to me, and have mercy on me, For I am desolate and afflicted.

The troubles of my heart have enlarged; Bring me out of my distresses! Look on my affliction and my pain, And forgive all my sins. Consider my enemies, for they are many; And they hate me with cruel hatred. Keep my soul, and deliver me; Let me not be ashamed, for I put my trust in You. Let integrity and uprightness preserve me, For I wait for You."
– Psalm 25, A plea for Deliverance and Forgiveness

When your actions are pleasing to God and you are doing what God your Father wants you to do; And when the splendor is the reward resulting from all your patience and perseverance in seeking to know and doing the will of God… whoa! It truly is a magical, soul stirring, heartwarming feeling that I want you to experience for yourself. But it's a journey. And it begins with simply taking the time right now in your life to pause, humble yourself, and taking whatever, it is that currently has priority in your life: whether it be work or TV or other people or clubs you're involved with… push it aside a little–condense its importance down while you put getting to know Jesus and seeking to connect with the Holy Spirit within your top priority. Remember… It's been there the whole time. You don't need to take a year off from school and backpack across the country from Hawaii to Alaska or live in the forest with gorillas to find oneself. You just need to open your heart to the Scriptures. This is another con of the devil that he has slyly infiltrated into the psyche of mainstream society. That when a young person is not quite sure what to do in life and where he/she belongs, the thing to do is to seek the answer outside of yourself and focus on the world, by traveling the world and filling your mind with new cultural experiences and beliefs to see what "feels" right, when actually–it should work the other way around.

"I am the light of the world. He who follows Me shall not walk in darkness but have the light of life." – John 8:12

Working through this book and committing to the exercises will help you find your true self by helping you in discovering and connecting to the Holy Spirit that lives within you and this is what will guide you to the path that God has planned just for you that will lead you to your destiny... no matter how far from it you've strayed. Remember what we read above in Timothy? It is the Bible and Holy Spirit that are your tools to transforming you into a truly complete, full, strong, powerful person. Not anything the world has to offer. This is how you "find yourself". It's not that difficult and there are no age, gender, or race restrictions. The devil's made us believe his lie that it's more complicated and that there's an age limit on this. Thinking back now...I realize it would have been a mistake if I had gone through with my idea to take my final semester off from school and go to the South Pacific as a Peace Corp volunteer. It "sounds" good and right and charitable but at that time I didn't know what I wanted to do in life. I wouldn't have been able to come up with anything if you had asked me to do journal exercise #1 at that time in my life because I had lost sight of my true self in trying to fit a mold. I wasn't mature enough. So, the Peace Corp seemed like a good stall move, and something I was "supposed" to do to "find myself". My intention to help was genuine, but there was also an underlying reason. I figured the Peace Corp was easier work and a shorter workday then any job in corporate America. And this sounded a lot more fun to me than life in a stuffy office working 9 to 5 with only a couple weeks off per year.

Now I can say with confidence and clarity that my gift from the Holy Spirit is compassion for the weary and suffering. Your true self will slowly be uncovered as your heart becomes less and less polluted by the evil world as it gets cleansed by the Holy Spirit. I can't wait to see where God leads us next. This is the step that is key in helping you to begin living and making decisions from that calm centered Spiritual place we talked about earlier. And from this place you will tend to make more decisions and choices in life that fit your true self and thus fall in line with your destiny so you won't help but begin to feel happy and confident in who you are and about how your life is unfolding, and this in-turn will bring you joy, contentment, inner peace, passion, and a courage even amid life's trials and tribulations. You'll go from feeling like nothing ever works out for you to feeling like everything is falling into place in its own due time. And the more familiar you become with your instruction manual and the more frequently you check in with your guide, the less likely you'll be to stumble or fall into the wrong path in life and the more you'll remain in control of your life. Isn't it interesting that society tries to convince us of the opposite? Society tells us that we're to make our own destiny / blaze our own trail and write our own instruction manual based on what "feels" right to us. And that we have ultimate authority over our own lives. And then when we stumble and fail–society looks down on us and tells us we're stupid and less than other people who have "made it". And then because this is our only sense of self-worth and how we gauge our success, now we don't like ourselves anymore, we feel as though we're not in control anymore. This is when we turn to drugs or other destructive behaviors out of self-hate and looking for something external to fill the void and make you feel better. But then this makes life tougher and more stressful than it was intended to be. The instruction manual is already written! Why do extra work that isn't even productive. And you don't have to blaze your path all alone if you stick close to your guide and heed the Spirits teachings.

There is an important element in society that we all need in order to be truly successful and to understand our full worth. And that is a connection with the Holy Spirit of God that lives within each of us and acknowledgment that the Bible is our instruction manual for life, given to us by God and reading and discussing the Bible openly in our homes as common practice. This is why I told you not to act on any thoughts or ideas or urges you have right away and to just write them down because until you have rebuilt your foundation and thought patterns based on the Bible and Holy Spirit you can't trust them.

> "I am the vine, you are the branches. He who abides in Me, and I in him, bears much fruit; for without Me you can do nothing. If anyone does not abide in Me, he is cast out as a branch and is withered; and they gather them and throw them into the fire, and they are burned. If you abide in Me, and My words abide in you, you will ask what you desire, and it shall be done for you. By this My Father is glorified, that you bear much fruit, so you will be My disciples." – John 15: 5-8

You've got to be willing to open your heart and seek out the knowledge and wisdom of Jesus. If those words–"Bible", "Relationship with Jesus Christ", "The Holy Spirit of God living in you" … make you feel anything other than joy and an intense immeasurable love… don't walk away just yet.

Do you have deep emotional scars and hold intense grudges toward a parent that didn't give you what you needed growing up or a teacher or system that failed to support you and give you the encouragement that you needed? When we hold another human being or way of life in higher regard and put man before God in our lives then we place all our heart and soul and trust and faith into other human beings. Then… when we get let down and hurt (it's not a matter of if–it's a matter of when and how much), each time this hardens our heart and we develop "thick skin", "build a wall around our heart" (as they say), as a defense mechanism for our emotional survival. Thus–we walk around putting on a front for the world… quick to be defensive… quick to strike first…brick by brick–layer on top of layer–sealing off our heart… so we don't feel the hurt and emotional pain. And then–wouldn't you know it… another lie the evil one has slipped into our culture is that having "thick skin" and being tough and not taking any crap from anybody kind of attitude is a positive thing.

No one is better than anyone else. No one. Not your parents–not senators–not celebrities – not the CEO of your company. Someone who's caved to the destructive temptations that try and snare us in life is no less of a person than anyone else either. But this is why we need to put God first in our lives by focusing on and putting all our trust and love and faith in Him who will never leave you and never lie to you. We are not supposed to walk around with "hard hearts" and "thick skin", with a big callous around our hearts. God needs to be able to get in and speak to your heart. God/Jesus is the perfect friend, the perfect father, the perfect teacher, and the Holy Bible is the truth that you can count on and rest your weary head upon and take refuge in all the days of your life.

Do you think the Bible will brain wash you? Is that why you keep it at a distance? Where do those thoughts come from? (head to heart or heart to head?). Think about it for yourself. The evil one has done a good job making our society believe we should put all our faith and trust in man… but then only to be crushed and left with a hard, calloused heart and a distrust for people and then this is when the pride, anger, jealousy and/or vengeance creep in and that "I'm gonna get mine" mentality. And then the evil one puts that doubting thought in your mind, "The Bible is written by men too, so you can't trust that either–thus you begin to think the Bible is something to be leery of and that participating in church functions and social group activities will make you look like a fool for believing those people. But now you know this thought is from the evil one. It's another of his lies.

> "Have you not known? Have you not heard? The everlasting God, the Lord, The Creator of the ends of the earth, Neither faints nor is weary. His understanding is unsearchable. He gives power to the weak, And to those who have no might He increases strength. Even the youths shall faint and be weary, And the young men shall utterly fall, but those who wait on the Lord Shall renew their strength; They shall mount up with wings like eagles, They shall run and not be weary, they shall walk and not faint." – Isaiah 40:28-31

Well, I must say–I am proud of you. Just picking up this book and peeking in, shows me you're seeking personal growth and your best life from here on out. And that you are not a week-minded, flavorless drone of a person. You felt lost and felt that desire for change and that gentle nudge from your Spirit… but unlike so many others who harden their hearts when they feel lost and rejected and stuck in a life and circumstance they don't want to be in – and then end up turning to food, drugs, alcohol, shopping, abuse, sex…etc. to cope by finding something outside of themselves to feel better and fill the void instantly; Which only serves in creating a false, temporary sense of joy–because this only buries and suffocates your Spirit even more to the point that your true self becomes lost and smothered out by all the destructive behaviors and unhealthy habits, and this results in you feeling even more miserable which puts you at risk for even more destructive behavior … or ending up that old bitter person with nothing but regrets to show for your life. Instead… you've softened your heart–a Spiritual response… the correct response (heart to head). You listened to that quite faint voice of your inner man. That voice that is buried at the moment under all the crap this world has dished out. Good for you for taking a step to do something about it and taking the initiative to free that voice. You've been doing it your way all this time and that hasn't worked out too great… yeah? So, you're looking to see if there is another way. And there is. You're discovering it now. I am so proud of you for getting this far. The great thing about God and the Bible is that they are always there, knocking on our hard hearts… waiting for us to answer. He won't hold a grudge, and He won't rub it in, and it doesn't matter how you look or how horrible you have been in your past or are right now, or how old you are or how much schooling you've had or what type of job you have, or how much money you make. He is a fisher of men. He casts his wide net and hopes that we realize we need saving and grab on. Lady's… He can be your knight in shining armor galloping in on a white horse to whisk you off your feet and take you away from all your stress and troubles, to live happily ever after as your guardian, your protector. But you must reach out and connect first.

The Connection

To get connected to the Spirit of God that lives within you, and to get back on the path that leads to your Devine destiny, it starts with reading the Holy Bible. Find a Christian bookstore in your area one day and buy a New King James Version of the Holy Bible. Aren't you curious by now to know more about what Jesus was all about, and to read the entire passages for yourself that I've quoted here? Aren't you curious… even just a little to try and understand God and experience what others feel when they say they have been "saved" or have "felt the presence of God". Don't be scared or embarrassed to walk into a Christian bookstore. Don't feel like you're going to open the Bible and all of a sudden become brainwashed into giving everything you own to a church or that it will make you stop going to the doctor because now, all of a sudden, you'll think that if you believe hard enough God will heal you. Or is your excuse that you think once you open the Bible you will begin to convulse on the floor and start speaking in tongues, screaming Halleluiah, Halleluiah, uncontrollably. If you are bitter or distrusting of religion, God, or the Bible, because of an experience in yours or someone in your families' life, for example, if a member of your family joined a small church in the back woods and they haven't been seen or heard from since.

For what ever reason you are nervous about or think that it will not benefit you to begin reading the Bible… it is another one of the evil ones' lies. He wants to keep you from the Bible as much as possible, because once you know the truth and experience the guidance of the Holy Spirit and realize your purpose and potential in life–it will be harder for him to convince you of his lies. It is the evil ones' mission to keep you as far from God and His guidance as possible. He's tricked you into thinking that the con artist pastor's and strange, cult religious groups that are out there are somehow related to God and the Bible. Pastors and church buildings are men and created by man. Remember the passage you read above... *"let no man glory in men"*. I'm not talking about getting connected to a church. I am talking about getting connected to God by getting connected to the Holy Spirit in you. This is your helper/your guide, that Jesus Christ suffered and died for you to get. Reading the Bible should be peaceful, quite time, spent alone with just you and your heavenly Father with no distractions, so He can reach the Holy Spirit buried in you and bring Him to the surface. If for what ever reason you still feel uneasy or uncomfortable about reading the Bible, analyze where these feelings are coming from–I think you'll find they're not coming from a place of truth but from an imaginative thought in your head. We tend not to trust things we don't understand or are unfamiliar with. Hasn't there been someone at your job or in your neighborhood that you just assumed was a certain way or that you just didn't like for no apparent reason... until one day you had to work with them, or you chatted with them for while and realized you were wrong about them. The mystery and distrust for that person slowly gets replaced with a warm, friendly, understanding feeling. The devil wants to keep us from knowing God and his Scriptures so we will distrust Him and put our faith in the wrong people and in the wisdom of this world. So, whose side do you want to be on? No matter how great and perfect a man or a woman seems–we are all still just human (even Oprah... or whom ever you hold in high regard). We can feel one way one day and completely opposite the next–depending on what new information we've received to change our minds. Your boyfriend may say he's going to go to church with you on Sunday but if between now and then his buddy offers him tickets to the football game he might change his mind. Wouldn't you rather put all your trust and faith into that which is proven consistent and never changing and all knowing? The Bible is never changing, and God always does what he says he's going to do. God never breaks his promises.

Don't start at the beginning of the Bible and try to read it like it's a fictional novel and think that you can just breeze through it quickly. If you start completely at the beginning and set the goal to read page by page cover to cover you will probably fail, because by the time you get into Genesis and get to the part about the son of Enoch born Irad; and Irad begot Mehujael, and Mehujael begot Methushael and Methushael begot Lamech and she is the mother of so and so who begot so and so ....etc. You'll be put to sleep with your head spinning. So, I don't recommend that strategy. Read the history of creation and the story of Noah and the Great flood in the book of Genesis, but then move on. The Bible isn't always easy reading so don't get overwhelmed with thinking you have to read the whole thing in a certain amount of time or even get through a whole page in one sitting and comprehend everything right away. There is no time limit. If you only read two passages a day or a week–that is fine. We're going for quality here, not quantity. I just want you opening the book as much as possible and really reading and analyzing and researching what you read. If you get to the bottom of a page and realize you were thinking about what you are going to wear tomorrow the whole time, re-read it. Before you open the Bible take a few deep breaths, and as you read the Bible pray–ask God to soften your heart and to show you what he wants you to know. Ask Him to show you the truth.

Journal Exercise #4: Read Matthew, Mark, Luke, and John. That's it... just the Gospels, (the first four books of the New Testament).

Read them again. And take your time this time. If the verse speaks of a particular place, take the time to go to the maps that are usually included in Bibles and locate the place and imagine what the journey must've been like. If you read a story in Matthew, see if the same story is in the other 3 books and compare the differences/similarities. Read the preface that is usually in the front of each chapter that explains the books of the Gospel and read the foot notes throughout the chapters. If you don't understand the meaning of something or a particular verse stands out to you, research these further by seeking to understand the time period in which it was written or by finding other areas in the Bible that touch on the same topic, so you get the full picture. Look up words in the dictionary that you don't understand.

Don't neglect exercises 1 to 3, now. These are cumulative. You should still be reviewing your list from Exercise #1, continuing to revise it to make it as precise as possible and to keep you reminded of those activities you genuinely enjoy–so you can pick something from the list when life starts to drag you down. From Exercise #2–once a week you should still be creating opportunities for bliss, growth, and splendor and journaling about them in the back of this book. Remember from Exercise #3 to jot down all of your ideas and plans for the future BUT DON'T ACT on anything immediately. Just keep working the exercises. As you get closer and closer to your destined path in life it will be easier and easier for you to weed out which ideas are the distractions, which ideas are visions of your future and which ideas you'll need to focus on at the current moment. But right now, all you should be doing in focusing on your Exercise assignments 1 to 4.

In Romans 12:2, it says, *"do not be conformed to this world, but be transformed by the renewing of your mind, that you may prove what is – that good and acceptable and perfect will of God"*.

Keep reading the Bible and keep seeking out Jesus and a connection with the Holy Spirit until you understand what this transformation means and feels like. This is the key to everything. When you hear things like: "all things will work out for good", or "ask and your prayers will be answered".

This only works if you've been transformed and can honestly say you are connected to the Holy Spirit living inside you and have a relationship with God through Jesus Christ. You'll know it when it happens. Keep reading the Bible and asking God to speak to your heart and give you wisdom and understanding.

God uses different verses to speak to us. Just like having a conversation with your family–you may say the same thing differently to your mother then how you say it to your sister. So different verses will be more significant and seem to speak directly to your heart that just goes right over the heads of others.

Here are some of my favorite verses. Did any of these make your Holy Spirit grow three sizes? It might end up being a verse that you've read 10 times already but just something about that 11th time....

"My son, do not forget my law, But let your heart keep my commands; For length of days and long life And peace they will add to you. Let not mercy and truth forsake you; Bind them around your neck, Write them on the tablet of your heart, And so find favor and high esteem In the sight of God and man. Trust in the Lord with all your heart, And lean not on your own understanding; In all your ways acknowledge Him, And He shall direct your paths."–Proverbs 3: 1-6

"Ask, and it will be given to you, seek and you will find; knock, and it will be opened to you. For everyone who asks receives, and he who seeks finds, and to him who knocks it will be opened. Or what man is there among you who, if his son asks for bread, will give him a stone? Or if he asks for a fish, will he give him a serpent? If you then, being evil, know how to give good gifts to your children, how much more will your Father who is in heaven give good things to those who ask Him!"– Mathew 7: 7-12

"Now it happened, as Jesus sat at the table in the house, that behold, many tax collectors and sinners came and sat down with Him and His disciples. And when the Pharisees saw it, they said to His disciples, Why does your Teacher eat with tax collectors and sinners? When Jesus heard that, He said to them, "Those who are well have no need of a physician, but those who are sick… But go and learn what this means: I desire mercy and not sacrifice. For I did not come to call the righteous but sinners to repentance."–Matthew 9:10 – 13

"If you were Abraham's children, you would do the works of Abraham. But now you seek to kill Me, a Man who has told you the truth which I heard from God. Abraham did not do

this. You do the deeds of your father. Then they said to Him, *"We were not born of fornication; we have one Father – God. Jesus said to them, if God were your Father, you would love Me, for I proceeded forth and came from God; nor have I come of Myself, but He sent Me. Why do you not understand My speech? Because you are not able to listen to My word. You are of your father the devil, and the desires of your father you want to do. He was a murderer from the beginning, and does not stand in the truth, because there is no truth in him. When he speaks a lie, he speaks from his own resources, for he is a liar and the father of it. But because I tell the truth, you do not believe Me. Which of you convicts Me of sin? And if I tell the truth, why do you not believe Me?"* –John 8: 38–46

"You are already clean because of the word which I have spoken to you. Abide in Me, and I in you. As the branch cannot bear fruit of itself, unless it abides in the vine, neither can you, unless you abide in Me. I am the vine, you are the branches. He who abides in Me, and I in him, bears much fruit; for without Me you can do nothing. If anyone does not abide in Me, he is cast out as a branch and is withered; and they gather them and throw them into the fire, and they are burned. If you abide in Me, and My words abide in you, you will ask what you desire, and it shall be done for you. By this My Father is glorified, that you bear much fruit; so you will be My disciples. As the Father loved Me, I also have loved you; abide in My love. If you keep My commandments, you will abide in My love, just as I have kept My Father's commandments and abide in His love. These things I have spoken to you, that My joy may remain in you, and that your joy may be full." –John 15: 3–11

"But when the Helper comes, whom I shall send to you from the Father, the Spirit of truth who proceeds from the Father, He will testify of Me. And you also will bear witness, because you have been with Me from the beginning."–John 15: 26–27

"But of that day and hour no one knows, not even the angels of heaven, but My Father only. But as the days of Noah were, so also will the coming of the Son of Man be. For as in the days before the flood, they were eating and drinking, marrying and giving in marriage, until the day that Noah entered the ark, and did not know until the flood came and took them all away, so also will the coming of the Son of Man be. Then two men will be in the field: one will be taken and other left. Two women will be grinding at the mill: one will be taken and the other left. Watch therefore, for you do not know what hour your Lord is coming. But know this, that if the master of the house had known what hour the thief would come, he would have watched and not allowed his house to be broken into. Therefore you also be ready, for the Son of Man is coming at an hour you do not expect."–Matthew 24: 36–44

"And it happened, as He spoke these things, that a certain woman from the crowd raised her voice and said to Him, Blessed is the womb that bore You, and the breasts which nursed You! But He said, "More than that, blessed are those who hear the word of God and keep it!"–Luke 11: 27–28

"Not everyone who says to Me, Lord, Lord, shall enter the kingdom of heaven, but he who does the will of My Father in heaven. Many will say to Me in that day, Lord, Lord, have we not prophesied in Your name, cast out demons in Your name, and done many wonders in Your name? And then I

will Declare to them, I never knew you; depart from Me, you who practice lawlessness!"–Matthew 7:21–23

God will communicate with you through the Scriptures to His Holy Spirit inside you and speak directly to your heart.

It's like this...say for example your job is to rent parking spaces. You work at the front desk, and someone comes in to rent a space at the end of a long day. You ask for their license, credit card and vehicle tag number. They say they don't have their tag number and ask if it's ok to not provide that information. In a tired, soft, non-confident voice you reply that you were trained to get this information but you're not sure why so you'll let it slide this time. You're tired and it's the end of the day and you don't feel like looking in the employee handbook to refresh your memory. You feel a little guilty but figure everything will be fine... you can't think of a reason why not.

Three days later when your manager is reconciling the cars in the spaces with the information on file you start to hear yelling coming from the back room. He's screaming about a vehicle that is in a space that doesn't have an owner in the system. The manager comes storming up from the back room with the employee manual in his hand–plops it down on the counter in front of you, jabbing loudly at a highlighted paragraph on the page with his finger saying, "We went over this in your training. You cannot rent a space without the vehicle tag number because this would make it easy for thieves to stash stolen vehicles in these spaces. And if such happens, then the establishment can be fined up to $1,000 for each day the stolen vehicle has resided here." He makes you read the paragraph out loud to him to make sure you got it. You feel bad now. You like and respect your boss. You don't want to be responsible for causing him to lose money to fines, all because you didn't follow instructions correctly. Twenty minutes later someone else comes in to reserve a space that also doesn't have the tag number of the vehicle. This time you don't have to think about it for even 1 second. You pull out the employee manual from under the counter and go right to the page you remember and say in a firm, confident voice while pointing to the highlighted paragraph. "I'm sorry–but section G: 14 paragraph 2 clearly states I'm not allowed to rent a space without verifying the tag number. Thank you–but I'm afraid I am unable to help you at this time." With the words of the employee manual fresh in your mind you can execute your job correctly, confidently and with fewer mistakes... thus less guilt. And your boss will be pleased with your work and give you rewards.

So... same goes if you read the Bible often. It's instructions for how to execute your life correctly, confidently and with fewer mistakes thus with less guilt, will be engrained in your heart. The more you stray from your connection to God and from the Bible the more mistakes and the more you may stray from the path of your destiny.

Satan is in the business of preventing the truth. He perverts the truth by:

- Denying the authority of the Scriptures. Then nothing matters anymore. Everything becomes based on individual preference or convenience.
- Denying Christ and God's gift of salvation.
- Convincing you that rebellion against Gods' will and His destiny for your life will work out better for you and be more fun.
- Oppressing people through their lusts.

- Creating doubt in Gods' word and Doubt in Gods' promises.
  http://www.christiananswers.net/q-sum/sum-g001.html

Let's Expose the Lies

The devil's Lie #1:

It's not necessary for us to seek out and put time and effort into following Jesus Christ and building a relationship with God. In fact, ... it isn't even beneficial to us. And those that choose to live the ol' high and mighty–praise the Lord–kind of life, are loony for choosing to do so, because that means they'll have to live a boring, poor, unsatisfying life, never being able to enjoy the finer things in life. The purpose of life is to "make it". And if you follow the following worlds' advice, you'll get "there":

> It's most important in life to put reading, studying and memorizing school books ahead of any church books or the Bible.
> You've got to seek out, pursue and sacrifice to get and keep the jobs that pay the most money in society.
> And you should spend your free time and thoughts trying to please and befriend the popular, influential, wealthy people so that they'll invite you to all their parties.

And if you do this... society tells us that this is the key to a happy, successful, easy life... right? Money, prestige, popularity, and all the perks that come with it. So, come on… join the "rat race"!

That is a lie that's been passed down through generations in society and pounded into our heads, burying the truth in our hearts. I think of the kid who worked so hard in school to get the job that someone else told him he should get. And the guy spending 80 hrs a week at the office trying to get that next promotion so he can buy a bigger house with a pool and get that luxury car. Or the kid who quits school because he's promised an opportunity to make a lot of money and after that first year the money dries up.

All following the false promise that fame or fortune or prestige will make you and your family happy and fill you with joy, peace, and contentment once you attain it.

Let me give you a scenario…

College scholarships are getting more and more competitive, companies have fewer and fewer openings, and the cost of living is going higher and higher. Parents want their children to be "successful", happy and to not have too much struggle in life. Thus, it's easy to lose sight of things we can not see in the natural world and get caught up with following what society and the media says is necessary to be successful and happy. And in a household where such is the case, the sole focus is grades–grades–grades–grades–good college–good college–good college–great career–great career–great career–more money–more money–more money. So, from 1st grade to 12th a child in this households' daily schedule is packed tighter than the Presidents. Doing homework, extra work, internships, running for offices, school clubs, going to extracurricular activities, playing 3 sports, entering writing, speaking, athletic, spelling bee competitions; A child is eager to please his parents and the attention from doing good in school and hearing his/her parents brag about how well they're doing and how great they are because they do well in school–it can become all consuming and the only focus in life and source of feeling good–and the end goal...the measure of whether this child will know that he's "made it" and is a success in life is that great six figure job. So... the child goes on to get accepted to a good college and continues to work really, hard–spending hours studying and memorizing facts and figures for tests and doing internships that will help get him to the next step and help him get that "good job". Graduation day is finally here the child feels glorious that all that work paid off and now there is just one more step... the "great career". The child goes on several interviews and accepts an offer with a company he really liked in the interview. It all seems great–it's almost over–a start day is set–he finally will have "made it". The parents brag to all their friends and family about how great their child is because he has a degree from this prestigious place and now a "good career", and about how the company has great benefits and how he's going to go on and get his Masters' and PhD next.

Three years latter...

At the end of a 12-hour day this child lifts his head up from his books–turns away from the computer screen for a moment and thinks...

"Where has all the time gone.... Is this it? Is this my reward for all the hard work and hours spent reading and studying, trying to be the best?...It was for this?...This can't be "it"... the reason for all of it?...This is such a disappointment ...I'm bored...I'm personally unsatisfied...this wasn't how I felt my life would turn out. Passionless–with no sense of real purpose...How did I end up here anyway?... OMG, I'M STUCK IN A MID LIFE CRISIS at only 26! Trapped. I feel like I'm suffocating. I have no idea what to do next. I feel completely let down by the world."

Because of the priority and the sole focus of this child's home life being based on the worlds' wisdom–the parents didn't realize it–but they were implying a promise to this child. A promise that said... if your sole focus in life is doing anything and everything necessary to get a good career (which is defined as one that pays well), and getting several letters attached to the end of your name–then you've arrived... then you can say "I made it, "I'm a big success in life". And everything will be wonderful and right with the world then. This will automatically make you happy because you'll be able to buy a big house and nice things.

This child fell for the lie and believed this empty earthly promise. Like all empty promises they will eventually let you down. They look pretty, perfect, and glittery from a far–but once up close and in the middle of it.... that's a different story.

Why is it some aspiring stars seem to be so grounded and well-rounded on their climb to the "top", but when they "arrive" ... once they've "made it" ... some seem to unravel. Maybe they fell for that false promise that tells us that if we become a famous star and everyone knows our name and we're in all the magazines and have so much money that we can afford our own personal jet and fancy houses all over the world–that our life will undergo a magical transformation and be wonderful and blissful and we would always be content and full of peace and passion because we could buy anything we wanted. But when that doesn't happen... I imagine they feel trapped, lost, suffocated in this world with no direction–and no idea of what to do next. Stuck, feeling let down by the world. And then even worse... they won't be able to complain to anyone because the rest of us who are still believing the lie are striving to "make it", and we're thinking... yeah right... if I had your money and star status–life would be perfect.

If we believe these lies and we're presented with the opportunity to lie, cheat, steal, murder or sell drugs for a lot of money, popularity, and prestige ... then I can understand why someone may do it. Because if all you've been told, all the images one sees, and all one believes is that this should be your main purpose and goal in life...if presented with an opportunity to try and skip a few steps to get there quick... then I can see why people feel like it's a no brainer to do it.

Do you tell yourself that if you could only win the lottery, then life would be great? You would have no more problems... then you would be happy. Do you daydream about all the stuff you would buy? You tell yourself you'll just stay bitter and mad at the world for your lot in life until you win the lottery. Because then ... then you'll suddenly be happy and generous, and your world will be a bright shiny place. This is a false promise. This is a lie used to keep you unhappy and ungrateful and mad at God and blaming Him and everyone else for you being stuck and having no joy in life.

This is what the White Witch was offering Caspian in the movie The Chronicles of Narnia: Prince Caspian. The White Witch represented the evil temptations of this world. When Caspian was at his weakest; drained, tired, faith weakened, and had lost hope–this is when she enticed him with the lie...she said, "One drop of blood and I can help you solve all your troubles. Only a prick of the finger and I can help put everything right." Just one little compromise and he would have power and prestige... the fight and struggle would be over. Temptations are even more enticing when our guard is down from either being too tired, too weary, too drunk, too angry, or too envious. But luckily, in the movie Peter has friend's whose faith is strong and his friends came to his rescue and reminded him to not listen to the Witch because she lies. Anything coming from her, no matter how enticing, would result in a life of regret and misery and only a short instance of bliss from the false satisfaction. His friends helped him to revive his Spirit and strength while he waited on Aslan (who represents Jesus), his true savior from the immediate struggles. And when Aslan showed up, he made everything ok and worth the wait and struggles. Which way would you rather have it? I know I would rather have a period of long suffering, persecution, and struggle if I knew it was for the truth and promise of true freedom, joy, and peace that I could trust in 2000%. Rather then take a risk on a shady character who promises all my fleshly desires will come true if I follow them and it will only require a few compromises.

Check out these verses in the Bible...

"Come to Me, all you who labor and are heavy laden, and I will give you rest. Take My yoke upon you and learn from Me, for I am gentle and lowly in heart, and you will find rest for your souls. For My yoke is easy and My burden is light."– Matthew 11: 28–30

"And He said to them, "Take heed and beware of covetousness, for one's life does not consist in the abundance of the things he possesses."–Luke 12: 15

"For what profit is it to a man if he gains the whole world, and is himself lost? For whoever is ashamed of Me and My words, of him the Son of Man will be ashamed when He comes in His own glory, and in His Father's, and of the holy angels."– Luke 9: 25-27

"Do not overwork to be rich;" –Proverbs 23: 4

"The fear of the LORD leads to life, And he who has it will abide in satisfaction; He will not be visited with evil." – Proverbs 19: 23

"When you give a dinner or a supper, do not ask your friends, your brothers, your relatives, nor rich neighbors, lest they also invite you back, and you be repaid. But when you give a feast, invite the poor, the maimed, the lame, the blind. And you will be blessed, because they cannot repay you;" – Luke 14: 12-14

"For he who sows to his flesh will of the flesh reap corruption, but he who sows to the Spirit will of the Spirit reap everlasting life. And let us not grow weary while doing good, for in due season we shall reap if we do not lose heart." – Galatians 6: 8-9

See… that wasn't hard to do was it…. go to the Bible for the truth and correction?

"If you love Me, keep My commandments. And I will pray the Father, and He will give you another Helper, that He may abide with you forever – The Spirit of truth, whom the world cannot receive, because it neither sees Him nor knows Him; but you know Him, for He dwells with you and will be in you, I will not leave you orphans; I will come to you." – John 14: 15-18

"But the very hairs of your head are all numbered. Do not fear therefore; you are of more value than many sparrows" – Luke 12: 7

So, the next time someone tells you, "This is what you need to be doing with your life...", or someone who starts making a little money off a get rich quick scheme that you turned down and now they're rubbing it in your face–calling you a fool. You should get a chuckle out of this because you and I know that what we really should be doing is what ever God desires of us and waiting on Him for our direction and next step in life. Quietly say to yourself..." just you wait...God's got great plans in store for me"!

Have you ever tried to put a big piece of furniture together from IKEA without reading the directions? You're going good initially in the beginning, everything looks like it's falling into place and that you'll be done sooner then you think...and then you run into a snag because the piece you now need, it turns out you used it already. What you thought was right previously, turned out to be wrong. So now because you're stuck... you turn to the instructions and realize you're going to need to pull everything apart and start over. In the long run–if you had just taken the time initially to read and follow the instructions from the beginning instead of trying to do it on your own, it would have been easier and taken less time.

This reminds me of life in our society. We think we can do it on our own and that it will turn out better and be more fun without following God's instruction manual for life.

Society tells us that Jesus doesn't need to be of high importance in our lives, and that we should listen to what the world says about how to "make it" in life and to follow our own individual desires and do what just feels right to us. But then what happens...society shows little help, compassion, or mercy to people when they stumble, fall, and end up lost from following this poor advice. We let the "justice" system charge children as adults even though I believe all scientists, and everyone agrees that a child's brain is not fully developed. It seems that if a respectable looking guy in a nice suit says–this child is just pure evil. The worst of the worst. He must be put away for life. You don't have to twist our arms...we'd rather they be locked up forever without the chance for parole–no forgiveness–no mercy–left to suffer the rest of their life in prison when loving instruction, truth and goodness may be all they needed from adults in society and we failed them. We're just too busy trying to please and conform to the world. When you get a chance, check out the movie "When Kids Get Life". And read the book "The Church of the Second Chance" by Jens Soering. This is a wonderful book that will make you think more deeply and cause you to question our cultural beliefs regarding inmates and the justice system in America.

"I was naked and you clothed Me; I was sick and you visited Me; I was in prison and you came to Me."–Matthew 25: 36

"Remember the prisoners as if chained with them – those who are mistreated." – Hebrews 13: 3

What if Peter in the Prince Caspian movie didn't have good Christian people around him to keep him strong in faith and on the right path. He might have given into the temptations of the evil one and his fleshly desire. Maybe not the first time… but if this was the only message, he was hearing…eventually he might be led astray. Like children growing up these days with out good leadership and teaching in the home and community… they are easily led astray believing a lie.

It's a good thing Jesus doesn't treat us like we treat each other half the time. No matter how long we go on working for the devil, perpetrating his lies, believing that we don't need

God, and that we can do life better on our own. God is there the whole time patiently waiting. And the second we turn to him and ask for forgiveness and mercy and acknowledge that his son Jesus died for our sins he gives us the loving correction and instruction we need.

"An eye for an eye", how many of us grew up with that one…? The belief that if someone does you harm or wrong or disrespects you, then it is your right to retaliate–pay back–give to him what he's got coming–teach him a lesson. These types of thoughts and beliefs…that are so engrained into the fabric and culture in which we live–are what I want you to question. Test everything you currently think or believe. Test everything EVERYONE says by searching your Bible asking God to show you the truth and the correct way of thinking. Keep reading… keep seeking until you find your answers.

Remember the Bible is your instruction manual–our rules of engagement for navigating this life.

> *"For the love of money is a root of all kinds of evil, for which some have strayed from the faith in their greediness, and pierced themselves through with many sorrows. But you, O man of God, flee these things and pursue righteousness, godliness, faith, love, patience, gentleness. Fight the good fight of faith, lay hold on eternal life, to which you were also called and have confessed the good confession in the presence of many witnesses. I urge you in the sight of God who gives life to all things, and before Christ Jesus who witnessed the good confession before Pontius Pilate, that you keep this commandment without spot, blameless until our Lord Jesus Christ's appearing, which He will manifest in His own time, He who is the blessed and only Potentate, the King of kings and Lord of lords, who alone has immortality, dwelling in unapproachable light, who*

no man has seen or can see, to whom be honor and everlasting power. Amen"–Timothy 6:10-16

Lie #2:
You're supposed to be saintly and a darn near perfect person with no flaws before you should begin going to church and getting involved in church activities.

The truth is that God wants you right now–right as you are, unconditionally. You could be in raggedy clothing, it don't matter. You could have gotten drunk last night, it don't matter. You could've had sex for drugs last night... God still loves you today and wants to build a relationship with you. You can still go to church today. You're not going to catch on fire if you walk through the doors. If you have been struggling with something personally like trying to kick a bad habit like porn or drinking way too much when you go out or abusing drugs or lying ... and you've told yourself that this is it... that this time you're making a change for the better to be a better person. And you've been going good for a while and then one day you just screw up–you give in and slip up. And now you feel ashamed, embarrassed, mad, and disgusted with yourself for not being strong enough and failing... again. The furthest thing on your mind at this point is to find a quite place, open the Bible, and begin reading the Gospels, and to speak out loud to God–telling God you're sorry for letting him down and to help give you the strength to fight your personal demons. Or to drive to a church and sit through a service. But this is EXACTLY what you should do! And EXACTLY when you should do it!! The world tells us that we're supposed to get ourselves "right", and then... when we're "good enough" we can go to church and talk to Jesus and others about God. If you tell someone you went to church... what might their reaction be... "huh – YOUUUU went to church!" Ha... that's a laugh. Let me step aside before you get struck by lightening". But this is the big lie. How do you know what the measure for "good enough" is? And you need God's help to "get right". The evil one wants to keep you down and struggling in a corner all by yourself fighting against him all on your own. This isn't a fair fight. The more communication you have with the Scripture and the stronger your relationship with God grows through the Holy Spirit, the stronger you'll be at changing bad habits and destroying destructive thoughts for good.

> *"And their scribes and the Pharisees complained against His disciples, saying Why do You eat and drink with tax collectors and sinners? Jesus answered and said to them, Those who are well have no need of a physician, but those who are sick. I have not come to call the righteous but sinners, to repentance."* – Luke 5: 30–32

It's like when a good friend or family member is mad at you and you two blow up at each other one day and get into this big screaming match and now haven't spoken in weeks because of this disagreement. The longer you go on not speaking to one another it makes the situation worse and tension more and more volatile. But what happens when you finally talk it out? You explain your side of the story, they explain theirs, and you discover that a few things people told you they said weren't even true. You both apologize and then hug it out and it's all good. Your friendship and bond is even stronger now. If you're mad at God because you feel like he didn't help you when you needed it and hasn't ever come through for you then instead of giving him the silent treatment and listening to what others have to say–sit down and talk it out with God over His Scriptures. Your friendship and bond will be stronger because of it too.

Lie #3:
Focusing and striving to do what's good and holy and being humble are negative characteristics. Being a proud, prideful person, someone who would never back down from a fight are good qualities.

"Who do you think you are acting all righteous and holier than thou?" Is what someone tells you when you try to tell someone they shouldn't do something because it's not right? And then we feel bad and apologize. End of story.

Say thank you next time and continue to discuss with them what the right thing to do is. It's human nature that we don't like to be judged. We don't like to be told what to do. Our pride doesn't like it. We want to be right and victorious and honored with accolades for our greatness. It's true that we ain't perfect and that we should be focusing on getting the plank out of our own eye before we go telling someone else about how they should remove the splinter from their eye. And I guess that's why we don't speak up when we see someone else doing wrong… because we don't want them to do the same to us and point out our bad qualities. But a distinction needs to be made here…

It is easier to see and point out what other people are doing wrong, then it is for us to do that to ourselves (that's the pride talking). But if you are coming from a place of sincerity, love, and encouragement to help another person from making a bad decision then it shouldn't matter if you have taken care of your own personal demons or not. We all struggle with different things. If you can help someone with their problem and can lead them to the truth in the Bible and help explain what God says concerning their specific issue–then you should speak up and say something. It's not your truth. It's not your personal advice...that's the distinction. You're just a vehicle to help lead that person to where they can find the truth and correction and the Godly wisdom in the Bible to solve their personal dilemma.

Are you seeing how the devil has twisted this one...? Nobody is perfect, yes–we all know this! And because of this we feel we can't tell anyone what they should or shouldn't do because we don't want to be accused of thinking we're holier than thou and that our poo doesn't stink. So, we just look the other way if we see someone else's kid going down the wrong path in life. And don't speak up if we notice a friend contemplating adultery. Keep your mouth shut if you witness someone steeling something or mistreating someone. If you tell someone they shouldn't steal. It's not your truth. That's not your rule. It's God's rule. We should tell someone they shouldn't steal and then be able to direct them to several scripture verses that give the truth and knowledge as why not to. Right! We shouldn't listen to other people. We should know that God's way is the truth and the right way. We should not be ashamed to point out to someone when they are doing something that is the opposite of what our instruction manual for life says. The manual is the same for everyone. But the world tells us that what is right and good should be decided by the individual and no other authority. We should direct people to the Bible and we should read the Bible ourselves asking God to show us the truth. Then it's between us and God if we choose to obey or ignore the truth. We'll have to answer to God if we turn away and decide to disobey God.

> *Pursue peace with all people, and holiness, without which no one will see the Lord: looking carefully lest anyone fall short of the grace of God; lest any root of bitterness springing up cause trouble, and by this many become defiled;* –Hebrews 12: 14-15

Lie #4:
Boys are easier to raise then girls.

This is a big lie the devil has hoped will cause parents to be more lax when it comes to raising boys. So that they'll succumb to their foolish youthful lusts. Think about it. In society it is somehow seen as ok and normal for males to be drunkards and practice fornication. It's almost like if a male doesn't do these things then he isn't seen as normal. Little self discipline and a tendency to commit adultery is somewhat expected from young males. And then we tell them they're supposed to be the "head of the household", and that that means providing money to buy nice clothes nice cars a nice house and paying to get their wives hair and nails and spa treatments done every week. This is a lie.

The truth is the most effort and the most teaching should be towards raising boys because boys should be taught how to correctly lead the family unit and what it means to be a true head of the household which is being a Spiritual leader and having the patience, self-discipline, and kindness to lead his family to love what is good and to seek out Gods guidance from the Spirit.

I think we all know the profound effects on both females and males of not having a father in the home or a father that's in the home but spends little time with his children... always working or too busy with his own personal projects or a father that's in the home but never shows encouragement or takes the time to teach and participate in his child's life and never provides positive reinforcement.

God made sure Jesus had a good father Joseph, who provided safety, security and protected what was good and right. It was Joseph the father whom God gave the instruction to move his family to Egypt to protect them from harm.

If you have boys, then you have a lot of work and a huge responsibility to train and instruct boys on how to be a good leader and future head of household which means enforcing that Jesus in control of the household. And the devil is going to fight you hard on this. Boys need to be taught that they should follow Christ and get to know the Bible and to keep their legs closed and to be patient, loving examples–because, as husbands, they have a big role to fill in making a good society.

> *"For the husband is head of the wife, as also Christ is head of the church; and He is the Savior of the body. Therefore, just as the church is subject to Christ, so let the wives be to their own husbands in everything. Husbands, love your wives, just as Christ also loved the church and gave Himself for her, that He might sanctify and cleanse her with the washing of water by the word."* – Ephesians 5:23–26

Boys grow up to be husbands and as husbands they need to know how Christ was head of the church, and how Christ loved the church so that they can mimic this behavior in their own families to keep the body of the family unit together. The Husband must know the Bible–the guidebook very well, in order to teach his family, the Word which renews the heart and cleanses the mind of evil thoughts. If our sons are taught what's right and what's good then they will be good husbands and good fathers, families will stick together, and daughters and sons will follow their daddy's lead. I guess its human nature, but it seems like a mother could be fighting with her child all day long to do something... whether it be clean up their room or finish their vegetables... and as soon as the dad comes home, he only has to say it once... and the child obeys. So, if fathers would put down the weed and the liquor and the video games and read the Bible with their sons and daughters and teach them that they should obey the authority of the Bible–this simple, easy thing to implement, would have a huge benefit.

And because this would have such a high benefit— do you see that a lot of the lies and false beliefs that the devil has infused into our society are geared more toward keeping males from knowing God and seeking truth in the Bible. Think about it...a man teaching a Sunday school class, a man sitting in a corner meditating on God's word, is not cool or seen as a "manly" thing to do in a lot of circles.

Thus, it becomes a vicious cycle. We're not teaching our boys what it truly means to be head of a household and what it truly means to be successful, the truly important things in life–thus they end up believing all the lies... which only leaves them feeling let down by society, confused and hating themselves because they feel like a failure if they don't "make it" according to the worlds' standards. So how can a man love his wife as himself when he hates himself because he was told being a real man means having a lot of money or being with a lot of females?

This Spiritually deprived man hurts the family unit, thus hardening the hearts of all people involved (the moms, dads, kids). Pride comes in then and builds up a wall to hide true feelings and to keep the heart from being broken again. But unfortunately, this also keeps the truth in the Word of God out.

So, then life and raising the kids become more and more of a daily struggle, thus less and less time is spent with sons and they'll grow up not knowing what it means to be a good Spiritual leader of a family–and so the cycle repeats itself.

Girls will always want to attract the boys and do what they think will please them for their love and affection and admiration. So, if a girl's father isn't setting this standard in the home and when girls look around in society and in the social groups around them at the standards from guys...if the message they see is that guys love girls who get drunk and make out with other girls and strip in clubs for him and his friends then girls will behave this way. But if majority of males in society are seeking a close relationship with God and striving to follow and be led by the Spirit in life and have the qualities of the Spirit: love, joy, peace, patience, kindness, goodness, faithfulness, gentleness, self-control.... Then girls will fall right in line and do the same with out much effort from parents because girls want to attract guys. But the way we're going now... with telling girls they should be the ones to keep their legs closed and be good wholesome church girls with Christ like qualities but then we send them out into the world where no guy or business is attracted to this... it's like devoting your life to telling a hen that pigs are the most handsomest animal in the barnyard and that hens should only seek to win over and date pigs and then send the hen out into the barn yard telling it to now... go make me some little chickens...." All your efforts would have been for nothing, because for all that effort the hen is going to need to attract and get with a rooster after all.

Then there're those lies that the devil uses against us individually hoping to find our individual weaknesses and snag us with one of them to bring us down; trying to keep us from developing a strong bond with God to hinder us from reaching our full potential. These are the lies I'm thinking about:

- You're not successful in life unless you're driving a BMW/Mercedes/Bently, have a Rolex watch on your wrist and Louis Vutton luggage and have a big house.
- It's important to be considered "cool" in high school. The popular people are better than you. You should be trying to be like them and do what they do.
- If you're smart and do well in school, then you should listen to everyone and become a doctor or engineer.
- What! You're 40 and you don't have a nice house or a nice car… then some thing is wrong with you.
- Because everyone in your family is fat, overweight, and out of shape, then you're pre-destined to be that way too. That's just how ya'll are–there is nothing you can do about it.
- Because you're a male you must look "hard" in pictures, you shouldn't smile. You don't want to look soft and corny. You must come across as tough. Gangsta.
- If you're a young male and you're not having sex or not into trying to get girls numbers and hollering at them when they walk by then you're gay.
- If someone does something to disrespect you, and you don't fight them or do something to retaliate… then you're a punk–you're soft.
- Because you're past a certain age you can't learn new things. Even though you're thinking about taking violin lessons or tap lessons …or something that has always been in the back of your mind as something you've wanted to learn. It's too late for that now… you're too old.
- Once you reach a certain age, females are supposed to gain weight and cut their hair short.

- Because you're female you won't be good at math or engineering or mechanics fields.
- If you're in a family and environment that all they do is either sell drugs or use drugs. Nobody has gone to college. Then that's what you should do too because that's all you know. That's probably all you'll be good at.
- The Bible isn't the authority on what is right and wrong and how one should live their life. It is up to the individual person to determine that for themselves. You need to experience everything and do what just "feels" right to you at the time. Those people that are all about the Bible and God are crazy.

"Behold, a sower went out to sow. And as he sowed, some seed fell by the wayside, and the birds came and devoured them. Some fell on stony places, where they did not have much earth; and they immediately sprang up because they had no depth of earth. But when the sun was up they were scorched, and because they had no root they withered away. And some fell among thorns, and the thorns sprang up and choked them. But others fell on good ground and yielded a crop: some a hundredfold, some sixty, some thirty. He who has ears to hear, let him hear!"–Matthew 13: 3–9

The word of God lands on all types of hearts.

Were the heart is hard satan can snatch away the word easily. Therefore, the devil has infused his lies into the culture of our society. So, we will have a world full of hard hearts and continue to stay separated from our Heavenly Father and from His love and wisdom and truth and our God given destinies and thus we'll start to devour our selves.

Many people say… "There must be more to life then this"? This is a little nudge from the Spirit hoping you'll take notice and search for Him. Yet… most of us don't analyze this thought more deeply. We just dismiss these thoughts as daydreams about a better life and then quickly put them out of our minds and tell ourselves it's hopeless and that we just need to settle for our lot in life even though it's uninspiring, mind numbing and soul grinding–never having a deeper introspective thought about Spiritual growth, and never pausing long enough to hear and appreciate the quiet, guiding, comforting voice of the Spirit.

Instead, the word is just snatched away, and we believe that lie stuck in our head that, "this is just my lot in life, there's nothing I can do. I'm just unlucky. Just gotta suck it up and take it. This is life." No. No… you don't have to take it. Don't be like other people that just give up searching for their "something more" in life and stop striving to reach their full potential. It's hard when you're doing it on your own… I know. It's one of those things that is easier said then done. Like trying to lose last 6 pounds. It is tough. But the show The Biggest Loser has shown us that anyone can do it if you don't give in and stay renewed in the commitment. Anything can be done. So, it's also possible–no matter where you are at this point in your life or where you came from, whether you're 9 or 90, you can connect with the Holy Spirit of God and identify the path to your destiny in life from this point forward. Staying connected to the Spirit and growing in the Spirit is key in helping you maintain the strength and commitment to stay on that narrow path during those times you grow tired and weary and the devil attacks with his enticing lies and false promises.

So instead of just watching the inspirational movies about true life individuals that came from poor, dark, troubling situations to become amazing success stories–pretend you're in a movie about your life and inspire yourself to begin reaching for your own amazing success in life. The exercises in this Journal will cultivate that good ground so when the word takes root in you... watch out. So, I hope you're giving it all you've got captain.

We live in a free society. We have a choice to live as a slave or to enjoy freedom. Yet a lot of us choose slavery. Why do we choose slavery? We don't even know that we're living as a slave because society doesn't talk about and debunk the lies in our culture and we don't take the time to read and discuss the instruction manual for life openly. I wish someone had told me about the importance of reading the Bible and that it is our instruction manual for life when I was growing up. So, I am telling you now. You have a choice to live as a slave and oppressed by your inner turmoil, negative thoughts, addictions, temptations, or to know what true inner peace and freedom is all about. Be careful that you don't choose slavery without even knowing it. Like the elephant that spent half his life chained to a pole–when the chain gets removed, he still acts as if he were chained... never moving further then 3 feet from the pole for the remainder of his life. Like that elephant... after we've lived a while in the "real world" and have been beaten up, battered, and bruised–we can choose to either submit and believe the lies society tells us to keep us chained down to earthly promises–or we can have a Spiritual revelation and be transformed by the Holy Spirit and bust out of those chains of bondage and begin receiving the knowledge, wisdom, and guidance from our Heavenly Father.

> *But then, indeed, when you did not know God, you served those which by nature are not gods.* – Galatians 4: 8

Stand fast therefore in the liberty by which Christ has made us free, and do not be entangled again with a yoke of bondange.
– Galatians 5

For he who sows to his flesh will of the flesh reap corruption, but he who sows to the Spirit will of the Spirit reap everlasting life. – Galatians 6: 8

We want God to work in our lives and change our lives for the better, right? We all yearn for something to happen in our lives that will give us concrete, overwhelming proof. A miracle. But the problem is… what we want and ask of God a lot of the time is a selfish, fleshly desire. It's God's will be done. Not ours. And He knows what is best for us. It's not like how we tell each other, "I got your back man". But don't really mean it. God truly knows what's best. The model prayer says, "THY will be done", not MY. And then we get mad at God and at the world when things don't go our way. That's your first test. First get in touch with the Holy Spirit and get to know God… then you'll see that He slowly changes the desires in our heart to match His plans for us. And THEN… when we ask our hearts desires. He answers and fulfills. Beautiful.

"This is an evil generation. It seeks a sign, and no sign will be given to it except the sign of Jonah the prophet. For as Jonah became a sign to the Ninevites, so also the Son of Man will be to this generation." – Luke 11: 29–30

We all know it deep down. But it's hard to just let go and trust God. This is because the evil one has been working on us for so long, sitting on our shoulder whispering his lies in our ear so seductively for so long–and with most of us not having anybody in our lives to point out the lie in our other ear–we don't even know we've been bamboozled–until we "hit bottom" and realize we'd been played by the evil world and left hanging. And now… when you hear the truth, you're not sure what to believe because your heart has been so hardened over the years. So, you tell God to show you a sign, and then you'll believe with all your heart. You want God to make the first move… "Show me" … is basically what you're saying to God. Well, Heeeelllllloooooo… God sent His only son to be persecuted and ridiculed and to die a painful, brutal, agonizing death on the cross for you. Isn't that enough for you… Geez. I bet none of your friends have ever done as big a favor as that for you. So, the problem is you then. You may say you believe in God and Jesus his only Son…but you don't truly, truly comprehend and believe it deep down. You haven't been transformed by the Holy Spirit yet then. Before moving on, repeat Exercise #4. Perhaps your issue is that you feel unworthy. You just can't fully believe that God and Jesus love you that much and were willing to sacrifice that much to cover your sins in full, and to provide you with a helper for life. Maybe God has been sending you signs and you're missing them or dismissing them because they're not exactly what you had in mind. Ask God to fill you with his Holy Spirit, and that you want to join his family and become a sister or brother to Jesus, and to guide you to recognizing the truth in the scriptures that will help you truly, truly believe with all your heart and all your soul that Jesus died on the cross for you.

"Also I say to you, whoever confesses Me before men, him the Son of Man also will confess before the angels of God." – Luke 12: 8

So, God doesn't need to give you a sign. It ain't his turn. Jesus made the last move...it's on you now. It's your turn. So, reach out–open your Bible–get connected to the Holy Spirit so you can find that path to your God given destiny. It will benefit you and glorify His name.

The more you read the Bible, the more the lies and the more the wrong way of thinking that you have believed in for so long begins to stick out like a sore thumb. What lies have you fallen for? Connect with me at www.ECEFit.com to tell me about it. Let's expose all the lies of the devil.

For each one of those lies that we've listed above... what if you were to do the opposite? You would get some funny looks from people, right? You know "the look" I'm talking about. You know the one. The head snaps back and cocks to the side, they look you up and down and side ways, with the Elvis lip, and the "hmmmm...who does she think she is", expression on their face. You know they're thinking... "what in the world is that person doing... don't they know they shouldn't be doing that because, <insert lie here>.

Let me give you an example...

- You're 50 years old and you tell your friends and family that you've started taking tap and drum lessons. Yeah... you'll get "the look".
- You've just graduated from college with a 4.0 gpa with a degree in Chemistry and pre-med. You decide to go on to Bible college to study to become a pastoral counselor. Yeah... you'll get "the look".
- You're a guy who grew up in a tough inner-city neighborhood. Belong to a street crew. Get in a lot of fights. Sell weed in the neighborhood. Then one day... you stop cursing, stop drinking, stop selling, stop hanging

out and start studying more, start getting good grades in school, get an internship, start dressing like a young professional, get accepted to a pre-med program. Yeah... you'll get "the look".

- Your family is over for the holidays visiting. Not a one of ya's is less then 250lbs. You get up in the morning and go downstairs where everyone is gathered in the kitchen chit-chatting and waiting on breakfast. You pull out turkey sausage, egg whites and buckwheat pancakes with flaxseed oil. Yeah... you'll get "the look".

Let 'em give you "the look" all they want. This is a good thing. We should all get those looks occasionally. If you've never gotten "the look" then correct me if I'm wrong–but you've pretty much done everything you are "supposed" to do in life according to the cultural box society has put you in. It's hard to get "the look", especially when it comes from your friends and family and fight the urge to give in and conform to the worlds view of how you should act or think. We're taught to fall in line, follow the leader, don't get in the way, and don't question the establishment. Remember lining up as a class in the hallway in elementary school to walk together as a class in single file line to the next classroom. If someone did anything as small as to put their arms up or do a little dance as they walked — the teacher would make the whole line stop and the child would get reprimanded. But we're supposed to be salt remember! Go ahead...shake things up... add your flavor!

I'm not saying that if you're not doing out of the ordinary, off the wall kind of things then you're not being your true self. You shouldn't do anything just for the shock value either. What I'm trying to convey is that we can't let what others think, or a preconceived stereotype about how we should behave or which path to follow in life based on our age, gender, weight, or ethnicity affect the choices we make in life. Once you've connected to your Holy Spirit and you have a clear understanding of what you need to do to get to the path that God has designed for you... then begin to step out and do what your heart and Spirit and prayer guides you to do, even if it isn't popular today or amongst your friends or family. To those whose path is less traditional or totally out of the norm for your culture then you'll have to stay strong and pull forth extra inner strength and power to fend against all "the looks" and negative comments you'll likely receive. What ever your path–don't let negative thoughts or sideways criticizing glances from others deter you from staying the course.

> *"Enter through the narrow gate; for the gate is wide and the road broad that leads to destruction, and those who enter through it are many."*–Matthew 7:13-14

> *"And I say to you, My friends, do not be afraid of those who kill the body, and after that have no more that they can do. But I will show you whom you should fear. Fear Him who, after He has killed, has power to cast into hell;"*–Luke 12: 4–5

I like that verse in Matthew about entering through the narrow gate. I think what is meant by it is that; it will be difficult to find your way in life with such a strong pull to be like everyone else. The devil has been so successful in manipulating this world into believe his lies. Therefore, God has given us the Instruction manual for life and the guide. For those who find the narrow gate along the narrow path that leads to your destiny and Gods will for your life it will lead you to your best life. So, the good ol' days aren't in your past. They aren't the carefree days of your youth. They are in your future. For His yoke is light.

Good for you for reaching out and exploring personal and Spiritual growth and pursuing your God given destiny. You are at a pivotal point in your life right now. It does not matter where you are at this stage in your life: how old you are, if you have a job or not, what your health is like. You have a choice right now, to begin today... always seeking, always searching, always growing in Spiritual wisdom and knowledge from the Holy Spirit and Jesus Christ and pursuing God's destiny for your life. Or... you can settle. You can choose your same old routine with your same old disappointments, and discontentment and fake joy. You can choose to believe societies promises and the lies of the evil one, or you can believe God's promises. Which side do you want to be on? You must decide. And if you're not working for God–then you're working for the devil. Imagine that God and the devil both appeared right now in front of you... wherever you are.

And each one said they had something they wanted you to do for them. God says, "I would like for you to _____". And then the devil says, "I want you to _____". Would you tell God No? But we do. We tell God no to his face so often and we don't even know it. We don't even recognize when the devil is slowly manipulating us–pulling all the right strings and getting us to bend to our fleshly desires.

To demonstrate what it will take to stay focused and determined; and the internal strength required to stay committed to continued growth in the wisdom and knowledge of the Spirit and to remain on the path that will lead you through the narrow gate... I have another exercise for you to complete.

Journal Exercise #5: Cleanse your body.

Here are a few options for you to choose.

[These diets are from the book "Dr. Jensen's Guide to Diet and Detoxification" by Dr. Bernard Jensen. I advise you to read this book before doing any of these cleanses and seeing a doctor or registered dietician for all of your health and diet questions and concerns.]

Option 1 (The 11 day Elimination Schedule) :

Days 1 to 3. To start your day, drink two 8-ounce glasses of water. After a half hour to an hour, have your first glass of grapefruit or orange juice, and continue drinking a glass every four hours. The reason I want you to use citrus juice is because it stirs up acids and toxins better than any other juice, and the water helps carry this unwanted material off. Remember to drink a glass of water every hour or so until you've had eight to twelve glasses. Take a hot bath before bed.

Days 4 and 5. Drink two 8-ounce glasses of water upon rising. For meals, eat fruit only, breakfast, lunch, and dinner. You may also drink juice between meals. Be sure you drink six to ten more glasses of water before going to bed. Take a hot bath each night.

Days 6 to 11. Drink two 8-ounce glasses of water after you wake up. For breakfast, take only citrus fruit. Between breakfast and lunch, you may snack on a non-citrus fruit. For lunch, have a garden salad with three to six different vegetables and two cups of vital broth. For dinner, have two or three lightly steamed vegetables and two cups of vital broth. You may use a little sea salt if you have it, or sprinkle a little vegetable broth powder on your veggies and broth for taste. Take a hot bath each night.

VITAL BROTH RECIPE

½ cup carrot tops
2 cups potato peelings
2 cups beet tops
3 cups celery stalk

2 cups celery tops
1 teaspoon vegetable broth powder
2 quarts distilled water
Onion for flavor

Finely chop first five ingredients, combine with vegetable broth powder and water in pan, bring to a boil slowly, simmer 20 minutes, strain, and use only the broth.

Option 2 (Grape Diet):

Four pounds of grapes a day is a good amount for a grape diet. These grapes should not be the seedless white or red grapes but the kind that have seeds since these are the most vital of all grapes. You can chew them fine if you like. A good thing to help eliminate catarrh is found in cream of tartar that surrounds grape seeds. You can go on grapes five to ten days without any supervision, but if you stay on them longer, it is advisable to have someone around who is familiar with the grape diet.

Option 3 (Watermelon Flush):

Going on watermelon for three, four, or five days can be a wonderful diuretic. We find that it helps to take out a lot of the debris in the colon, and the extra water picks up toxic materials and carries them off.

This exercise will take some planning on your part as to when would be the best time for you to begin. Don't begin the cleanse during Christmas or on your birthday or during a time when you know you're going to go to Six Flags...but once you start…commit to finishing. This means that if a co-worker bakes your favorite cake from scratch or brings in your favorite cookies or birthday cake to celebrate someone's birthday… you'll have to say no thank you. If your sister calls you crying and wants to talk over lunch… you can only drink water or eat according to your cleansing schedule. Your sister is going to look at you like your cheese done slid off your cracker (especially if you're known for liking to eat). You'll get "The Look" several times during these 11 days and you're going to want to cave into the pressure but once you start, Do Not Break the diet. There will always be something. An excuse for why you must stop. But see it through to completion. The lesson you'll learn and benefit from this exercise is that (1) you'll prove to yourself that you do have the inner strength to accomplish something even though it's exceedingly difficult. (2) You'll learn to feel comfortable looking people in the eye and telling them no… no thank you. Even though the thought in your mind is telling you to give up and stuff your face with that cake. (3) Although you'll grow weary from the peer pressure and tired from the caloric restriction … you'll realize that you can dig down to a deeper level and pull from your Spiritual inner man the inner strength that you didn't know you had to make it through the tough temptations, and you'll feel good about yourself when you make it to the end. (4) Physically you will feel really, good because your digestive system will be humming like a well-oiled machine not having had to work overtime digesting all the excessive fat and carbs.

Let no one deceive himself. If anyone among you considers himself wise in this age, let him become a fool so as to become wise. For the wisdom of this world is foolishness in the eyes of God. So let no one boast about human beings. – First Corinthians 3:18-21

I know that just getting through the day right now may be a struggle for you. It might be tough because, either you're just plain miserable and depressed about your current situation and still have no idea how you're going to dig out of the mess you're in, or you've been through all the exercises up to this point and you've had a breakthrough and you're pumped and inspired, full of the Holy Spirit and have an inner drive and clear picture for the direction your life is meant to take–and you're ready to begin making changes in your life but you also know that it's going to be a long road ahead and that you'll have to be patient because it will take time to reach the point when you can begin to really start to take the first steps toward that new path in life. So now everyday just feels forced and fake–like you're running a marathon that's been uphill the whole time and you're waiting and waiting and waiting…to reach the top so you can coast for a bit. You're moving forward but every inch feels like a mile right now, I know. You're thinking to yourself that if you don't reach the top in the next few months you don't know how much longer you can keep climbing. You want to just give up and quit trying because it's been all up hill so far and it's hard and you're running low on energy and inspiration and you're having moments of doubt, thinking that maybe the peak just isn't attainable for you–maybe you're just not good enough and not one of the lucky few after all.

This is why you have the journal exercises. For continued inspiration and renewing of the Spirit, to help you stay on course and to carry you through the tough days and around the stumbling blocks that your enemy will use to try and keep you from reaching that path.

Just look to this day...worry only about creating entries of, "Bliss from Growth", "Glory from Action" or "Splendor from achievement" for this day. Then each new day do the same thing and before you know it... you'll be right on out of your current situation and into a better place where you can coast for a bit. Where life won't feel so forced and fake anymore and you won't have to work so hard and the internal struggle that zaps all your energy will be gone, because your new situation will feel good, feel confident, feel right. Then showing the world your light and giving it your salt will come more naturally.

This reminds me of that movie "Walk the Line", with Joaquin Phoenix and Rease Witherspoon. Johnny Cash was struggling there for a minute. It was a daily struggle for him when he was lost and had no internal peace and was struggling with his personal demons. For a time there, it was like he was walking through the thickest of rain forests... but then found himself on a paved road. Imagine the relief and freedom of being able to walk normal and not having branches and spider webs hitting you in your face and tripping and falling and looking at the ground before you take a step so not to step on a snake because of all the vegetation in your way and not being able to see further then two feet in front of your face–and then, all of a sudden, stepping onto a road. When Johnny Cash got free from the bondage of drugs–it was like he stepped out onto this road... his path. He had a moment of clarity and his destiny became clear. God was right there waiting for him. And his destiny was in line with his God given gift for entertaining. And his life seemed a lot easier for him then–he appeared more confident and more at peace with himself. And this was the reason he was able to stand firm in his decision when he told the record label people that he wanted to perform in a prison. They gave him "the look". (see what I'm talking about... "the look")–but he stood firm and didn't conform. As you begin to grow in the knowledge and wisdom of God and you get connected with your Holy Spirit and experience the power and euphoria and strength and confidence that comes from knowing that God is in you and that He's got your back...you begin to completely fall in love with yourself and embrace your past and all the wrong turns and bad choices–because the now feels so good... you would do all the bad all over again if you knew that was the only way to get to now. You'll understand it then–that the Holy Spirit is a wonderful blessing from God, your Father. If someone offered, you a winning lottery ticket or the Holy Spirit of God which would you take?

In the end we all cherish the good times spent with our earthly fathers and not the money he's spent on us. We should want to have memories of good times with our Heavenly Father also. And as a result–you will start to be bold in the face of temptation. You'll feel free to be yourself because you know God has your back. If you were a kid getting bullied in elementary school–wouldn't you stand up for yourself more if your cousin who is a champion boxer came with you to school one day. Well... what if God him self was with you?

> *"For I say, through the grace given to me, to everyone who is among you, not to think of himself more highly than he ought to think, but to think soberly, as God has delt to each one a measure of faith. For as we have many body parts that make up our body, but all the parts do not have the same function, so we, being many, are one body in Christ, and individually members of one another. Having then gifts differing according to the grace that is given to us, let us use them: if prophecy, let*

us prophecy in proportion to our faith; or ministry, let us use it in our ministering; he who teaches, in teaching; he who exhorts, in exhortation; he who gives, with liberality; he who leads, with diligence; he who shows mercy, with cheerfulness."
– Romans 12: 3 -8

Let's stop taking the easy route folks by conforming to one of the man-made templates for life that this world has created. These are usually based on economic status or which neighborhood you came from–or your age, gender, or race. God doesn't care about those things. But it's up to you to care enough to connect to the Holy Spirit and build a relationship with God so God can communicate to you His plan and your true destiny in life.

Wide is the path that leads to destruction. It's like a scene from a campy horror movie? When the girl is running through the haunted house and comes to a dead end. She frantically looks around for an escape as the tension grows because you know the monster is closing in on her. Then all of a sudden, an elevator door opens wide–giving her an option for an escape route. This is the easiest choice to make. The elevator door is wide open, just sitting there waiting. If she doesn't take it the other option is tougher. She'll have to turn and face the monster. She decides to get on the elevator — the doors close — the lights go out and the elevator descends into the monster's liar for an easy meal.

Your correct path in life is through a narrow gate. And depending on how long it's taken you, it might be covered with moss and overgrown shrubs and vines. It's only wide enough for one... YOU! You won't be able to hit auto-pilot because there are going to be a lot of twists and turns and ups and downs–you're going to need to stay vigilant, so you don't drive off a cliff or get distracted and veer off your path. The ride will be the best experience of your life. Along the way you will be shaped and molded and continually growing into the person God wants you to be. And it will be a million times more rewarding then if you just take the template offered to you by the world. It's tempting I know… when all our friends and peers are following a pre-set path and seem to "have it all". Don't fall for the false promises, and the facade.

The True Promise

If you're thinking you're done... that you've "made it"! That you're a "success" in life. And your measure of success–what you've been chasing this whole time was money and a nice car and a nice house, a prestigious job, being the best at what you do and having the respect of your colleagues (the best wide receiver... the best actor...etc), having the best clothes, are the perfect size and having vicious shoes. If this is the foundation of your happiness and satisfaction... then watch out... because that house is about to crumble any minute. Worse than the little pigs house built out of straw, this house is built out of hot air. The devils' hot air.

    Until you can say you have a personal growing relation ship with God, are connect to the Holy Spirit and are like Jesus (meaning you are like the person he was when he lived here on earth...sinless), then you have NOT "made it". You can not claim you're a success. Of course–we can never live up to that statement. And that is the point. It's like an internal checks and balances system. What is it people say...'"? Once you're at the top–it's all down hill from there–so enjoy the journey while you can". These are people believing the lie. If my idea of the "top" is having $500,000 in my bank account–then sure I can get there quick by going out and robbing a few people and selling a few drugs... BAMM! I'm there. Whoo Hooo! I made it!! And yes–I better enjoy it quick because the police will be at my door any day now to take all my "success" away. The true "top", the true measure of "success" isn't reachable for us humans born of the flesh. So, there should never be a downhill. We should always be seeking–always be striving–continually growing in the knowledge and wisdom of God and learning and allowing God to train us and mold us to be like Jesus and allowing God to do His work through us. So, from now until the time of your death, enjoy the journey. "Bliss from growth", "Glory from Action", "Splendor from Achievement" should become a never-ending cycle of your life.

The movie "Notorious BIG" depicts exactly what I'm trying to tell you here about the illusion of success this world tries to feed us. Watch this movie. It is wonderful!

Material possessions and perishable items should not be the most important thing to us–it doesn't matter how many degrees or cars or houses we have–None of that is more important than the current state of your inner man and your relationship with God. Staying connected to your Spirit and following God's path for your life by reading the guidebook (the Bible) and listening to your helper (the Holy Spirit), is what matters most in this life. But in this fast passed–superficial society, we don't slow down long enough to get to that deeper level and appreciate it. Just because someone has a prestigious degree, a high paying job, 2.5 wiz kids, a perfect little dog, a perfect house with a perfect yard–that doesn't mean they are all grown up and doing well in life. The true measure of a man and a woman is how much they've grown and are growing personally and Spiritually with God.

And unfortunately, there isn't a quick test for this, as this world would like. Only God can judge. Because only he knows a man's heart.

If we refer to the instruction manual, it tells us how to deal with this.

"We shall know them by their fruits".

Do you know what I mean when I say that "after church feeling"? Come on …. You know what I mean. Don't you feel all warm and fuzzy inside after church on Sundays? The to-do-list which was top of mind walking into church–suddenly doesn't seem all that necessary anymore. Don't you want to feel that "after church feeling" most of the time? And not just on Sunday's. It's peaceful right…? And that's what we want–right?

So, there's a disconnect here. I guess we think that "after church feeling" is just a passing, "feel good moment", and that the real deal is the lie that if we sacrifice for money, fame, and fortune we'll find permanent peace and happiness. Or that living that 'party all the time' lifestyle is the real fun and joy.

The **true promise** that we can put all our trust in and believe with our whole heart, is that building a relationship with God through Jesus Christ and growing in the wisdom of the Bible and the knowledge of the Holy Spirit–leads to true inner peace, joy, passion, purpose, contentment, and a transformation that will feel magical, even during roadblocks, snags, and trials that life will throw at you.

"The LORD is on my side; I will not fear. What can man do to me? The LORD is for me among those who help me;"–Psalm 118: 6 – 7

"Happy is the man who finds wisdom, And the man who gains understanding; For her proceeds are better than the profits of silver, And here gain than fine gold. She is more precious than rubies, And all the things you may desire cannot compare

with her. Length of days is in her right hand, In her left hand riches and honor. Her ways are ways of pleasantness, And all her paths are peace. She is a tree of life to those who take hold of her. And happy are all who retain her. The LORD by wisdom founded the earth; By understanding He established the heavens; By His knowledge the depths were broken up, And clouds drop down the dew. My son, let them not depart from your eyes – Keep sound wisdom and discretion; So they will be life to your soul And grace to your neck. Then you will walk safely in your way. And your foot will not stumble. When you lie down, you will not be afraid; Yes – you will lie down and your sleep will be sweet. Do not be afraid of sudden terror, Nor of trouble from the wicked when it comes; For the LORD will be your confidence, And will keep your foot from being caught."–Proverbs–3: 13 – 26

"*Whoever trusts in the LORD shall be safe. Many seek the ruler's favor; But <u>justice</u> for man comes from the LORD."–* Proverbs 29: 25 – 26

"*Wait on the LORD; Be of good courage, And He shall strengthen your heart; Wait, I say, on the LORD!"–* Psalm 27:14

"*See, I have set before you today life and good or death and evil, in that I command you today to love the LORD your God, to walk in His ways, and to keep His commandments, His statutes, and His judgments, that you may live and multiply; and the LORD your God will bless you in the land which you go to possess. But if your heart turns away so that you do not hear, and are drawn away, and worship other gods and serve them, I announce to you today that you shall surely perish;"*– Deuteronomy 30: 15 – 18

"And the LORD, He is the One who goes before you. He will be with you, He will not leave you nor forsake you; do not fear nor be dismayed." – Deuteronomy 31: 8

"Fear not, for I am with you; Be not dismayed, for I am your God. I will strengthen you, Yes, I will help you, I will uphold you with My righteous right hand."–Isaiah 41:10

"For He who would love life And see good days, Let him refrain his tongue from evil, And his lips from speaking deceit. Let him turn away from evil and do good; Let him seek peace and pursue it. For the eyes of the LORD are on the righteous, And His ears are open to their prayers; But the face of the LORD is against those who do evil."–Peter 3:10-12

You're going to be out and about visiting with friends or family one day and someone will say something, or something will happen that will be the complete opposite from what you just read in the Bible a few days earlier. You're going to remember reading it because it was one of those verses that just stood out to you. It's going to eat you up inside because you'll try and remember the exact wording, but it just won't come to you. Or at least not as eloquently as it was stated in the Bible. You'll go home and try to find the verse in the Bible, so you'll know it the next time, but won't be able to find it. It's awesome that the words of the Bible are in your heart, but when this happens it's frustrating. Especially if you want to explain to someone what it was that you read. And if you piece together your thoughts and try to explain it in your own words, it probably sounds extremely annoying for the person on the receiving end who doesn't know God or even own a Bible, if you say it like, "I read in the Bible somewhere that that's wrong." It sounds like it's coming from you. As if you are the judge and jury. So, while you're reading the Bible and come across sentences that are particularly intriguing to you–write down the subject, book, chapter, and verse where it can be found. This way... the next time you can pull out your journal and say, "You know what... I read something in the Bible the other day concerning just this subject. Matthew 6: 14 says, "For if you forgive men their trespasses, your heavenly Father will also forgive you." And you can show them your notes or even better if you have a Bible with you offer it to them to read it for themselves. This way it isn't your opinion that you're stating–you're just sharing exactly what you've read in the Bible, which is everyone's instruction manual for life. No offense in that. It's like that game telephone. From the time you read the verse to the time of the moment that reminds you of it, and you are trying to recall it, you might leave off a few key phrases that you felt weren't important to you but might make all the difference to someone else. Or–we may not be able to resist the urge to slightly change the context to fit our needs a little more. For example, if I was reading the Bible in bed and my husband were laying next to me. I may be reading a whole chapter silently to myself and let's pretend a line say, 'A husband should always massage his wife's feet before bed if she is with child.' Well... I might have the urge to say, "Honey... I just read in the Bible that a husband should always massage his wife's feet before bed."

So, we should all study and get the truth from the Bible for ourselves with our own eyes.

You know how if you watch a movie a 2nd and 3rd time different things stand out to you that you didn't catch the other times you watched it. You understand the meaning more and more each time and pickup on little things that you didn't notice the first time. Things you thought you knew—you end up realizing you understood it wrong. The same goes for the Bible. And if you've had a particularly hectic day or you're busy and you just pick up the Bible and rush through a few verses quickly to fulfill your assignment—you're going to miss a few of His promises.

> *How remarkable that the God of the universe would actually want to communicate with us! We are creatures of a material, physical world to which we relate through our five senses. God is a Spiritual being. We in our physical state cannot see him, hear him, or touch him, so how can he communicate with us? Through the Bible.*[2]

The Bible is a wonderful history and reference book. It teaches the history of this world they don't touch on in schools. The Bible tells how the good news of Jesus Christ spread through out the world and how the early churches began. There are even drawings of country boundaries during this time and the routes taken by the men who set out to spread the word about Jesus outlined in the Bible. Think about how brave those people must have been. There is even a dictionary in some Bibles to look up meanings of words. It's amazing to think about how bold and brave the followers of Christ were during

---

[2] *From Godsdailypromises.com which was adapted from the TouchPoint Bible with devotional commentary by Ron Beers and Gilbert Beers, Tyndale House Publishers (1996)*

this time. This must have been a challenging task. We can all imagine how barbaric the times probably were back then. They didn't have freedom of the press and freedom of speech. The original supporters of Jesus risked their lives to spread the news about the life of Jesus–and yet it seems as though today, we are slightly scared and even embarrassed, to bring up Jesus or God or the teachings of the Bible openly in our daily lives and conversations, even though most people would say they believe in God and go to church (at least on Christmas and Easter). Think about what those men probably went through, traveling in a world where Christianity wasn't even known or accepted yet. But that is probably why God choose them–because he knew they were up for the job. Let's pay them their respect, humble ourselves and at least seriously read the Bible.

All the parables and exciting stories that you'll find in the Bible, will amaze you at how much they apply to life today. You'll do a double take to make sure you're not reading a book written this year. It's unbelievable. So, if you've been doing it your way this whole time–then I'm sure you've learned a few lessons out the hard way. Have you come across those teachings in the Bible yet? I bet when you do/did–you said to yourself... Awh maaaaaan–this could've saved me a lot of struggles and mistakes in life. I wish I had read that earlier. The devil is happy that the relevance of the Bible has been diminished today. He wants you to go it alone–because he knows you'll stumble, fall, hit a brick wall eventually–and he's hoping you'll fall so far and believe so deeply in the empty promises of society, that you'll harden your heart so much–that you'll never humble yourself, never come to know God and never know His peace and love and guidance and truth, thus never reach your true Destiny. The Bible is your reference book, and the Spirit is your guide through life.

Our bodies originated in the soil of Eden. It should not surprise us that they are sustained by food that grows from the soil. Every source of food ultimately finds its nourishment in the soil, and that nourishment sustains our bodies.

Likewise, our souls were created by the breath of God in Eden; it should not surprise us that the Word of God, which is inspired, or "God breathed," sustains our souls. If we plan to eat food each day to keep our body alive, shouldn't we also plan to feast on God's Word each day to sustain our soul?[3]

As you read the Bible and come across passages that inspire and stand out to you–use the pages in the back of this book to jot down these verses and their subject matter–so you can find them later. Once you've accumulated several versus you might find it helpful to read these each morning before you start your day or before you go out for the evening.

"For there is not a just man on earth who does good and does not sin. Also do not take to heart everything people say, Lest you hear your servant cursing you. For many times, also, your own heart has known that even you have cursed others."– Ecclesiastes 7:20-22

After Matthew, Mark, Luke and John → read Proverbs, Job, Psalms, Ecclesiastes, Acts, Peter and then the letters of Paul: Romans, 1 Corinthians, 2 Corinthians, Galatians, Ephesians, Philippians, Colossians, 1 Thessalonians, 2 Thessalonians, 1 Timothy, 2 Timothy, Titus and Philemon.

---

[3] *From the* TouchPoint Bible *with devotional commentaries by Ron Beers and Gilbert Beers, Tyndale House Publishers (2003), p 649*

We don't hesitate to buy tell all books from celebrities or ex-presidents. We do this to get an inside look into the person they really are. We want to understand their thoughts and understand why they did the things they did. Well... don't you want to understand your God too, the creator of all things? As you start to read more and more of the Bible and grow in the wisdom and knowledge of the Spirit–you'll start to understand more and more who Jesus was and how God thinks, how he operates and what he wants you to do to help him. Reading the Bible is very comforting. Like a big warm hug from a loving father. The perfect father. We all have two fathers, the one who made us in the flesh here on earth and our Father in heaven. Our earthly fathers aren't perfect, they must deal with the same temptations and struggles of life that we all do and as a result will have certain areas that could use improving. Your father in heaven is perfect, *"When my father and my mother forsake me, Then the Lord will take care of me."*–Proverbs 27:10. And the Bible is everything that he wishes to say to us and to teach us. No matter how old you currently are, you are still a child of God and he yearns to embrace you and to teach and tell you all the things a perfect, loving father would.

This is what so many of us long for. And this, you can count on being steadfast, always there and always relevant throughout your whole life. Different chapters and verses in the Bible inspire and resonate differently with different people. Because God knows each one of us individually and He knows each of our needs–He knows He may have to say something to someone one way and say it a different way to someone else, for both people to get the same message. God's parenting of us never ceases. He's constantly teaching us lessons that sometimes may be painful to go through–but it is only for our own good. But just like how we try to avoid our earthly fathers when we're trying to get away with something, we know we aren't supposed to do... this world has been trying to get away with doing it's own thing and satisfying fleshly desires and evil thoughts–thus society and popular culture has been avoiding God and Jesus.

The Mourning Period

People say the mark of a true Christian... someone who knows God and is doing his will–is someone overflowing with Joy, peace, and happiness. This is true. However–especially in the beginning when you have that big Ah Ha moment and you're filled with the Holy Spirit and all of a sudden you realize that you've been bamboozled by the devil and that you've been believing all the false promises of this world for all these years and that God has been there the whole time wanting to love and be closer to you but you've just now realized it and you're wishing you had realized this earlier in life... I think it's normal to go through a mourning period.

When you finally go to Christ, for real, and acknowledge that you've been in the wrong and ask him to forgive you of your sins and to have mercy on you and that you want Him to work in your life. When that amazing feeling of the Holy Spirit and the grace of God comes over you and the fog clears and you realize what an idiot you've been–this is such a humbling experience that you become so thankful to God, and feel so blessed to have received the Spirit–that this may also be accompanied by an immense feeling of guilt and sadness. Guilt for the way you've been living your life all these years, living in the dark not acknowledging God when Jesus did all that for you. You may feel so un-worthy and so undeserving of God's love. Like a little child who feels sad when they disappoint their Father.

And realizing that now you are part of God's family and that it was your sin that your brother Jesus died on the cross for…; I think it's perfectly ok to go through a time of mourning, aloneness, and a period of sadness for your old self because of the wasted years you spent trying to do it your way when you could have been spending all that time with God and Jesus. And sad for all your other brothers and sisters in Christ all throughout the world that you know are suffering in poverty, persecution or in prison. But you're here now. And that's what counts.

But don't pull away from God and stop reading the Bible during this time. The devil will play on this doubt in your head and make you think that you are so unworthy of this much love and of the Holy Spirit–that you may be tempted to stop here and to slide back to your old familiar self and old way of life and thought patterns. After living in misery and hopelessness for so long, one can grow accustomed to it and comfortable with it. This grace from God and feeling powerful and feeling that the sky is the limit is something new…you've never experienced these feeling before–you don't know what to expect next.

You're not the same person anymore–God has stripped away a few of the bad layers–so this is an adjustment period. But remember God is always there to help you. This is when you need to lean on the words of the Bible even more. Keep seeking, keep knocking, keep reading, keep drawing closer to God. Your past does not dictate who you are now, and where you can go from here – now that you are walking with God. Stay vigilant. Remember from Exercise #1, there's that iron curtain keeping you from going back to your past anyhow… so let's keep moving forward. Think about how much better life is going to be now that you have a relationship with God, now that your heavenly Father is apart of your life and you've been sealed by the Holy Spirit to help guide you through life and to help you avoid the stumbling blocks.

"Therefore, submit to God. Resist the devil and he will flee from you. Lament and mourn and weep! Let your laughter be turned to mourning and your joy to gloom. Humble yourselves in the sight of the Lord, and He will lift you up." – James 4: 7, 9-10

God has wonderful plans in store for you. You'll emerge from this mourning period a stronger person. More in touch with your true self and more connected to the Spirit. With a new foundation for your life–the strongest foundation you can have, that will sustain you through any storm life may throw at you–and God will make sure nothing breaks your foundation. But now we must build on the foundation. God will shape and mold you into the man or woman He wants you to be so He can do his works through you.

This is exciting stuff and exciting times! Instead of focusing on gaining material wealth and social status and trying to please people–get a new focus on doing what pleases God and trying to always live in the Spirit. And this will lead to the joy and enthusiasm of a Christian filled with the Holy Spirit.

Building Healthy Habits

"Beware that you do not forget the LORD your God by not keeping His commandments, His judgments, and His statutes which I command you today, lest – when you have eaten and are full, and have built beautiful houses and dwell in them; and when your herds and your flocks multiply, and your silver and your gold are multiplied, and all that you have is multiplied; when your heart is lifted up, and you forget the LORD your God who brought you out of the land of Egypt, from the house of bondage;" –Deuteronomy 8: 11-14

Once you have established a relationship with God and know that the Spirit is working in your life and you can say that you honestly believe now and you're feeling good about yourself and your situation. Don't stall here. You'll want to keep growing, keep reading the Bible and keep asking God to continue his work in you so that you don't forget and end up falling back into old bad habits. So, let's build healthy habits that will keep us renewed with Gods love and grace.

Journal Exercise #6: Think about God all through out your day. Acknowledge Him in everything and give him praise.

We agree that it would be great to be led by the Spirit and feel that "after church feeling" during the week and not just on

Sundays after church–right? Well let's not just talk about it–let's be about it. How can we be led by the Spirit throughout the workday if we never even give God a single thought through out the whole day and when something good happens to us we get all puffed up with pride and pat ourselves on the back?

If you get a good performance review at work and get a bonus–immediately give God thanks for the recognition. Donate 10% of that bonus to a good charity or a person you know who is in need that may not have a job that provides them the opportunity to get bonuses.

If a solution to a problem that you've been working on for days suddenly pops into your head–immediately give God thanks for His help and kindness.

If you go to a concert and have a good time–give God thanks for having the ears to hear and the means to go and enjoy such wonderful creativity in this world.

If a new neighbor moves in next door and you're not getting along too well–give God thanks. Thank Him for giving you this opportunity to grow and practice the principle of walking in the Spirit and being kind and understanding to your neighbor even when he may not be kind to you.

If there is a co-worker at work, you don't get along with. Perhaps you like to see the glass half full and they are always seeing things half empty. As soon as they do something that rubs you the wrong way and you just want to give them a piece of your mind–stop and immediately give God thanks for this co-worker, as this will be an opportunity to practice patience and love. Ask God for ideas on how you can build a positive working relationship with this person.

If money is tight and it's looking like you won't have enough to cover all the bills this month and you start to worry and begin to really feel anxious–stop and give God thanks for what you have and for this opportunity to show Him that you remember the scriptures and that you are going to obey his commandment to not worry because you know the heavenly Father knows what you need, you'll seek and focus on the Kingdom of God instead of worrying about tomorrow.

This is hard to do on a daily basis, all throughout your day, especially when it's not something you normally do. You may get home from work and realize you never thought about God once all day. So that means you made several decisions, spoke to several people, made several judgments throughout the day and the Spirit was never brought in. God should be a part of your everyday life. Not just for a moment on Sunday and then it's back to relying on human wisdom and fleshly desire during the week for the important stuff. Thank You, Thank You, Thank You God for all that we have, for all the blessings you've given us. Thank You: For sending your son Jesus to die for our sins, and for your overwhelming love & forgiveness, thank you for the Bible, thank you for this wonderful country, and thank you for the gifts you've given me. It may take a while before you get into the habit of including God in every day thought life. It might help to subscribed to email messages from godsdailypromises@leftbehindprophecy.com. If this is still available at the time you're reading this, they send short lessons from the Bible with verses and prayers to your email that you can read and re-read during your day to help you stay inspired and centered and keep God foremost in your mind.

From the time you wake up in the morning to the time you go to bed at night, speak to God often and listen for his guidance and quiet reassurance. Here are some suggestions on what you can say:

"So, He said to them, when you pray, say: Our Father in heaven, hallowed by your name. Your kingdom come your will be done on earth as it is in heaven. Give us day by day our daily bread. And forgive us our sins, for we also forgive everyone who is indebted to us. And do not lead us into temptation, but deliver us from the evil one."- Luke 11: 2–4

God–I am asking for your help, wisdom, understanding and guidance today LORD. Guide me to the path and through the narrow gate that you desire for me. Help me to make the right choices. God, give me the understanding to be able to hear your voice and be obedient to your commandments and to not give into temptations and my fleshly desires. God, continue to work on me to make me a better person. Use me. I want to help someone else. In Jesus' name–Amen.

God–forgive me for being too wrapped up in my own personal life, and my 'To Do List' that I ignored you today. If there was something you wanted me to do today and I ignored your prompting–forgive me God. Forgive me for loosing my patience and getting frustrated today. Don't give up on me. I want to do your will. Thank you so much for everything you have given me: my health and my job…etc. Show me what it is you want me to do and which direction to go? In Jesus' name–Amen.

I am tired and weary Lord. Revive my Spirit. Renew me. Refresh my mind LORD. In Jesus' name–Amen.

Finding a local group and learning some meditation techniques may be valuable to you as well. Or for additional inspiration read Sanskrit quotes from the Hindu faith. Type up short inspiring quotes and Bible verses and place them in the pockets of your jeans or jackets. Then when you wear them, you'll surprise yourself with bursts of inspiration.

"You have received the most valuable human body, which is like a strong boat to take you across the ocean of maya. It is propelled by the favorable wind of God's grace and steered by the Spiritual Master. If with all this facility a soul does not cross this ocean, he is spoiling the golden opportunity he has received." (Bhagwatam, 11/20/17)

"You have been blessed with a human birth, which is difficult to attain. Don't waste the precious moments of your life in pursuit of sensual pleasures." (Shankaracharya)

(Above quotes are from: http://www.bhakti-yoga-meditation.com/inspirational-quotes-sanskrit-aim.html)

Psalms is a beautiful book. Choose a psalm of the week–that you read each morning when you wake up or each night as you lay in bed. I love reading soothing Psalms before bed. It's like being rocked to sleep. I like Psalm 54.

Journal Exercise #7: Surround yourself with positive/uplifting/inspirational music.

You must keep a strong, continually growing relationship with God to find and stay on the path to your true destiny in life. Music by-passes your head and just goes right to your heart and soul. I love music. When it's positive and inspirational and reminds me of Gods love and His Greatness…it just melts my heart and takes the stress and temptation away.

In addition to reading the Bible, Prayer and reading inspirational quotes–surround your self with inspirational music. Some songs I like for this are:

The Commadores – "Jesus is Love"
Eminem – "Not Afraid"
Yolanda Adams – "Never Give Up"
Carrie Underwood – "So Small"
Rodney Atkins – "If You're Going Through Hell"
Yolanda Adams – "I Gotta Believe"
Van Zant – "Help Somebody"
Prince – "All that Glitters"
Jimmy Cliff–"I can see clearly now"
Josh Turner – "Long Black Train"
Martina McBride – "Blessed"
The All-American Rejects – "Move Along"
Brooks & Dunn – "Believe"
India Arie – "Strength, Courage, and Wisdom"
Jimmy Cliff – "You Can Get It If You Really Want It"
Jimmy Cliff – "Roots Women"
Eminem – "Lose yourself"
James Fortune & FIYA–"I Trust You"
Michael W. Smith – "This is your time"

    A lot of songs you can turn into being about God. If a lyric in a song says, "I can't live with out you." I'm thinking in my head, "I can't live without you God. I love you so much…". Use your journal to jot down songs you hear that you want to download later and add to your inspirational play list.

    I don't care who you know. No one…no one, can give you the blessings and protection that God can. So why do we try so hard to please man, and only think about God in our spare time/ occasionally, on Christmas and Easter. We need to change our priority. Hopefully by now, it has changed for you already. We should put God first all the time no apologies. If you must distance yourself from some friends or family members currently in your life that are holding you back, then do it. This will give room for you to spend more time with God so He can mold you into a better, more complete person and then introduce you to new friends. I heard Joel Osteen say on his TV show one day, "Pigeons travel in flocks–Eagles soar alone."

If your best friend has been there for you your whole life. But if every time you try an explain to him or her that you've found God and that he's transformed you into a new person and that you're not the same person you were before and that this amazing change is happening within. Maybe the old you, used to spend $200 just on drinks for you when you went out. You'd close the bar down and know everybody's name in the place before the night was over. But now ... you just want to enjoy a couple beers with friends over dinner and fun conversation and then go home early. But instead of supporting and helping you–your friend looks at you like you're lopsided... orders you two jager bombs–and says "Nawww .... I know you... you haven't changed... come on man... drink up". And before you know it–it's 3:00am and you've just confirmed what your friend said. The next morning you wake up frustrated and angry because you know (and God knows) that that behavior is not truly you anymore. It's sometimes best to create some distance for a time being so you can continue to grow. Even if it's from your own family. If as soon as you walk though that door to your Moms house–you regress back to your 15-year-old self and your mother starts treating you like your 12 again and this makes you regress back to old self sabotaging behaviors, and then it takes you a day or two to get back to your calm, centered Spiritually mature self after the visit. It might be best to limit these situations until you're more solidified in your new self and even more connected to the Spirit, when you're further down your path.

Journal Exercise #8: Exercise

Take your inspirational play list from Exercise #7 and listen to it while you workout. Working out doesn't have to be stressful or awfully long, and you don't need to spend money on joining a gym. You can start with something as basic as committing to spend 10 minutes doing jumping jacks every morning when you wake up. Or jumping rope.

Look on www.fitnessmagazine.com to get exercise moves and motivation. Find a local park where you can begin walking or jogging 3 days a week while you listen to your inspirational music. Cable comes with excellent exercise programs on demand. Some vitamin shops have free magazines that provide exercise routines that you can do at home.

Exercising and getting fit is empowering. If you push yourself and get through those last 5 minutes on the treadmill even though you want to stop, then you can also persevere and continue to build a stronger and stronger relationship with God despite the pressure the evil world will put on you to give up. And you don't want to limit Gods options for what He can do with you just because you're unfit and out of shape. We want to stay healthy for God so He can use us anywhere to do his will and so we can enjoy life and the fruits of our labor to the fullest. Record in your journal the days when you exercise and what you did.

Tests and Trials

When Jesus was alive on earth his life wasn't exactly a walk in the park Kazansky, so we shouldn't expect ours to always be easy and work out exactly as we want, when we want it–we ain't better then Jesus. Besides... that would be boring. Bliss from growth feels darn good, doesn't it? And sometimes, that growth comes from making it through tough, trying, turbulent times and coming out wiser/more confident on the other side, realizing God was using this as a teaching moment.

I'm thinking about the story of Jonah and the Whale. Jonah didn't obey God's instruction to him to go to the city of Nineveh to warn the people to change their wicked ways. God loved even the people of Nineveh, but Jonah despised the people of Nineveh, so he didn't want them to turn for the better and be saved by God. Jonah tried to run from God, but God caused hardship and tribulation to come into Jonah's life to teach him a lesson. Jonah lived 3 days in the belly of a fish. This experience humbled Jonah. He prayed to God for help, repented and praised God.

God kept Jonah alive and gave him a second chance. This time Jonah obeyed and went to Nineveh and did what God asked. God is so good. The experience ended up being an amazing growth filled experience for Jonah. He became a better person for it.

I'm thinking about the story when Jesus preached to Peter and the others on the boat and then told them to fish again, after they had fished all night and hadn't caught anything. This was a test. Peter obeyed Jesus and put the nets back out again. The nets nearly broke they were so heavy with fish! And Peter felt the bliss from growth in the trust of Jesus that day.

Let's reflect on the tribulations and tests you've endured and been through in your life.

Remember that other person you used to be before you were a member of Gods family and before you had the wisdom and knowledge of the Bible and realized your gifts from the Holy Spirit. Do you remember all those days… months… years that went by with you never even giving God a passing thought? You went all that time missing out on a relationship with your Father in heaven, and not knowing his unconditional love and guidance. Remember when you were struggling to overcome your personal demons on your own–and how God just took it away in an instant the second you truly repented and acknowledged what Jesus did for you. Remember when you were measuring how good you were, and your self-worth based on that flimsy temporary joy from acquiring material possessions. And that it would eventually fade… and then you were left feeling empty… and the cycle would repeat… you wanted to feel that "joy" again so you'd strive to get even more money so you could buy more.

"For what will it profit a man if he gains the whole world and loses his own soul?–Mark 8: 36

I'm proud of you. You've come a long way. I know you don't want to go back to the old you. I know you want to continue growing in the knowledge and wisdom of Christ so you can inherit your victory that God has promised you. Now is your second chance. You're at the beginning of a whole new path; the narrow path that will lead to your Devine destiny. You're a new person. And this time you have your Spirit guide and God on your side.

> *"Now then, we are ambassadors for Christ, as though God were pleading through us: we implore you on Christ's behalf, be reconciled to God. For He made Him who knew no sin to be sin for us, that we might become the righteousness of God in Him."* –Corinthians 5:20

> *"For you are the temple of the living God. As God has said: I will dwell in them and walk among them. I will be their God, and they shall be My people." Therefore Come out from among them and be separate, says the Lord. Do not touch what is unclean, and I will receive you." "I will be a Father to you, and you shall be My sons and daughters, Says the Lord Almighty."* –Corinthians 6:16

I'm sure several ideas that you started out with in Journal Exercise #3 have been crossed out. The ones that remain should fall in line with Gods direction and what the Spirit is nudging you to do. So now follow. Respond.

** WARNING **

Be alert! Now, more than ever – the evil one will try his hardest to get you to give up, throw in the towel and go back to the old you if not worse. He is always looking for a little crack in your armor to squeeze in his doubts. He knows that you are closer than you've ever been before to God and reaching your God given destiny–so he will put in overtime to throw all kinds of temptations your way. He's looking for you to have a weak moment and then overload you with guilt and then overload you with thoughts of unworthiness or doubt or just the thought that you're too tired to go on any longer. This is a trick to try and get you to give up and go back to the old person you once were–living in the flesh. It may get so tough that you'll begin to question why I am even doing this–it may be mentally draining at times. You'll feel like you're swimming upstream a lot of days. But this is when you can rely on the journaling exercises in this book to keep you on track and moving forward and out of your head.

God is looking for a few good men and women. He wants to see if He can trust you to carry out His will and obey His instructions and not give in to the evil world the second you feel a little stress or peer pressure. They don't say fight the good fight of faith for nothing. They use these strong words because to follow Gods will and to stay on the right path that leads to your wonderful destiny takes strength. The inner strength of faith, courage, and wisdom. That path is narrow–and it's going to be a bumpy ride. So, make a mean face–growl a little–stomp your foot and get determined to face these tests with drive and determination, eager to prove to your Father in heaven that you are ready to be trusted with your first mission. Journal exercise #8 on exercising is not primarily about looks on the outside. On those days when you think you can't jog another minute on the tread mill, but you stick it out and complete the whole 30 minutes. This makes you stronger physically and emotionally–and gives you the confidence and character to complete another tough task in another area of your life.

Make a note in your journal that the book of James is for help during trials.

Profiting from trials

"My brethren, count it all joy when you fall into various trails, knowing that the testing of your faith produces patience." – James 1: 2-3

Loving God under trials

"Blessed is the man who endures temptation; for when he has been approved, he will receive the crown of life which the Lord has promised to those who love Him. Let no one say when he is tempted, "I am tempted by God"; for God cannot be tempted by evil, nor does He Himself tempt anyone. But each one is tempted when he is drawn away by his own desires and enticed." – James 1: 12-14

Qualities Needed in trials

"So then, my beloved brethren, let every man be swift to hear, slow to speak, slow to wrath; for the wrath of man does not produce the righteousness of God." – James 1: 19-20

God is going to test your faith by the diligence of others. I love that line. We'll see how long your promise to God to stop cursing (or what ever it may be) lasts when there is someone that just keeps nagging and nagging and pestering you…

Change your priority, to focusing on doing what pleases God (your heavenly father), for your personal satisfaction. You will feel 100x more special and get more satisfaction from knowing that you are doing what God wants you to do, than from any retaliatory vengeance you inflict on another. When we do what we know is pleasing to Jesus, we in-turn feel better about ourselves our life, we're more confident because we're one step closer to being the person God intends us to be. This indirectly makes us perform better at work and in life. Then you'll witness the promise… all things work together for good for those who love the God.

> *"Therefore do not cast away your confidence, which has great reward. For you have need of endurance, so that after you have done the will of God, you may receive the promise:*
> *For yet a little while, and He who is coming will come and will not tarry. Now the just shall **live by faith**; But if anyone draws back, My soul has no pleasure in him.*
> *But we are not of those who draw back to perdition, but of those who believe to the saving of the soul.*
>
> *Now faith is the substance of things hoped for, the evidence of things not seen. For by it the elders obtained a good testimony. By faith we understand that the world was framed by the word of God, so that the things which are seen were not made of things which are visible.*
>
> *By faith Abel offered to God a more excellent sacrifice than Cain.*
>
> *By faith Abraham obeyed when he was called to go out to the place which he would receive as an inheritance.*
>
> *By faith Sarah herself also received strength to conceive seed, and she bore a child when she was past the age.*
>
> *By faith Moses, when he became of age, refused to be called the son of Pharaoh's daughter.*

By faith the walls of Jericho fell down after they were encircled for seven days.

By faith Noah being divinely warned of things not yet seen, moved with godly fear, prepared an ark for the saving of his household." – Hebrews 10: 35-39, 11: 1-7

What will be your demonstration of faith? Listen and wait on the Lord.

"Therefore we also, since we are surrounded by so great a cloud of witnesses, let us lay aside every weight, and the sin which so easily ensnares us, and let us run with endurance the race that is set before us, looking unto Jesus, author and finisher of our faith, who for the joy that was set before Him endured the cross, despising the shame, and has sat down at the right hand of the throne of God. For consider Him who endured, such hostility from sinners against Himself, lest you become weary and discouraged in your souls. You have not yet resisted to bloodshed, striving against sin. And you have forgotten the exhortation which speaks to you as to sons:
My son, do not despise the discipline of the LORD, Nor be discouraged when you are reprimanded by Him; For whom the LORD loves He disciplines every son whom He receives.

If you endure discipline, God deals with you as with sons; for what son is there whom a father does not discipline? But if you are without discipline, of which all have become partakers, then you are illegitimate and not sons. Furthermore, we have had human fathers who corrected us, and we paid them respect. Shall we not much more readily be in subjection to the Father of Spirits and life? For they indeed for a few days chastened us as seemed best to them, but He for our profit, that we may be partakers of His holiness. Now no chastening seems to be joyful for the present, but painful; nevertheless, afterward it yields the peaceable fruit of righteousness to those who have been trained by it.

Therefore strengthen the hands which hang down, and the feeble knees, and make straight paths for your feet, so that what is lame may not be dislocated, but rather be healed. Pursue peace with all people, and holiness, without which no one will see the Lord:
Looking carefully lest anyone fall short of the grace of God; lest any root of bitterness springing up cause trouble, and by this many become defiled; lest there be any fornicator or profane person like Esau, who for one morsel of food sold his birthright. For you know that afterward, when he wanted to inherit the blessing, he was rejected, for he found no place for repentance, though he sought it diligently with tears." – Hebrews 12:1-17

"Let brotherly love continue. Do not forget to entertain strangers, for by so doing so some have unwittingly entertained angels. Remember the prisoners as if chained with them – those who are mistreated – since you yourselves are in the body also. Marriage is honorable among all, and the bed undefiled; but fornicators and adulterers God will judge. Let your conduct be without covetousness; be content with such things as you have. For He Himself has said, "I will never leave you nor turn away from you." So we may boldly say:

The LORD is my helper;
I will not fear.
What can man do to me?"
- Hebrews 13: 1-6

This just puts it all into perspective, doesn't it? When you think you're having a bad day and you're not even sure if you can make it through the day–read this to help put everything into perspective. Be thankful your daily struggles are not to bloodshed like Jesus. And be thankful if you're not suffering in a real prison right now like some are... unjustly. When you feel trapped in your daily routine, hopefully this scripture will help you to keep pressing on, to get you through. I know this helped me when I was halfway through writing this book and my computer crashed and I lost the file.

Rejoice in the midst of these trials, they are for the purpose of molding you into becoming–like Christ: more patient, more compassionate. And this is when you could say you've "made it".

Do you remember reading Greek mythology in school and thinking that it would be cool to be half human half God? They have the favor of the Gods and seemed to be a little swifter, stronger, and smarter than others–and they would go out on valiant quests and prove their greatness.

Guess what... this is you.

God is in you. And he has a quest for you to seek your destiny.

That path of your quest is narrow–just wide enough for one. One wrong step to either side and you're off the path. You need to stay vigilant and keep checking your manual (The Bible) often to make sure you haven't gotten off your path and aren't accidentally following someone else–or trying to have one foot on the right path and one foot in another path. We can't be drunkards and gluttonous eaters of meat because this makes us sleepy and lazy. We'll snooze one too many times and find ourselves veering off course. And just like those last 5 minutes on the treadmill seem like the toughest. Stay healthy so you can enjoy your victory.

An excellent movie to watch when you feel like you can't continue much longer is "The Power of One" with Morgan Freeman and Stephen Dorf. It shows determination and perseverance.

The character Stephen Dorf plays wouldn't have been as strong in overcoming the burdens and pressures of assignment had he not been strong physically as well.

I hope that if I were a member of the ruling class in South Africa during apartheid that at least I would have silently resisted. I hope that if I were a member of the ruling class during the segregated and lynching South I would have been involved in the march on Washington. I hope that if I was a member of the ruling class in a country that was practicing genocide, I would have helped try to hide people or spoken up to try and end it. I hope that if I were a member of the ruling class when the Indians were forced to leave their lands that I would have spoke up against it. I hope that if I were in that crowd that crucified Jesus under pontious pilot that I wouldn't have just followed the crowd and condoned it. And I hope that when my faithfulness to do Gods will is tested that I don't flinch and that I don't give in–no matter how big the temptation.

The Victory

Congratulations. You're on your way.
You're serving God... therefore God will show up to serve and guide you. And with God by your side, anything is possible.

I realized that there are so many opportunities to grow Spiritually and to help people right where I am. God may want you to be a friend to someone at your current Job. The job you felt so trapped and miserable in before...may now become full of purpose.

The meaning of life is to try to live your life as Jesus did–exactly as God is calling you to do.

In Mark, Chapter 12 Verse 30 it says the first commandment of all is to love the Lord your God with all your heart, with all your soul, with your entire mind, and with all your strength. And the second is you shall love your neighbor as yourself. There is no other commandment greater than these.

I don't think there are many of us that can honestly say we have mastered these commands. Even those with the "best" jobs, the most money and prestige. And this–is the criteria that determines whether we have "made it".

If everyday we're striving to live as this verse commands and we never stop pursuing a closer and closer relationship with God then, we are a success in life.

Reach out to me at www.ECEFit.com, to let me know how you have changed that is more pleasing to God. I'd love to hear from you.

I feel the reason for all the dark times, badness, and bitterness in the world toward others and ourselves like: Abortion, Drug abuse, Alcohol Abuse, Physical Abuse. Is because we don't have a close relationship with God and are not in touch with listening to our inner man, the Holy Spirit within us. Think about it… If you were doing what you **100%** knew, deep down was what you were supposed to do… that it was what God was calling you to do – we all would be at peace and overflowing with joy. You would have no reason to abuse others, or escape the trapped feeling through drug abuse, or bring a gun to work to shoot your ungrateful boss or be emotionally brain dead because you're stuck in a career that isn't right for you.

But you have grown from your experiences over these past several days, months, years while working on your Journal Exercises. You've had the BIG Ah ha moment! But externally… perhaps nothing drastic has changed. To the outside world you may look and seem the same. For example, say you run into an old friend from high school and chat for a few minutes (reminiscing); he wouldn't immediately pick up on how you've grown Spiritually, and that you've connected with the Holy Spirit and that you've gained Godly wisdom. I say this to make the point that we don't really know anybody… only God truly knows someone. Only he knows the inner man.

Thus, you don't know when someone else has had their BIG Ah Ha moment. You could leave work one day come back the next to a boss that may be a totally different person with a new Godly perspective on life because they might have had a profound realization the night before while reading the Bible and now, they too are at the beginning of a wonderful

Spiritual journey. So, let's strive to always be encouraging to one another–because we don't know where others are in the journey of their life. The man who cleans your toilets at work might be closer to God and Spiritually more mature than the pastor of your church. Only God truly knows a man's heart. A pastor is tempted just like everybody else (maybe more so). He might have given into greed, lust and envy a few years back but because he built up such a loyal good church back when he was on the path–now out of pride and shame he's covering up his indiscretions to maintain that front. But God knows. And what happens in the dark will eventually come to light. Your faith isn't in people or in a building, your faith and trust is in God and the Bible. If you have faith and trust in a person, it isn't that person in the flesh–you have trust that the Spirit of God is working through that person to fulfill a Godly purpose.

Who's to say Jesus is not going to come back in our lifetime... within the next few years... tomorrow even. Why are you so sure he's not coming back in your lifetime? If you say you believe in God and that Jesus Christ died for your sins and that he will come again to judge the living and the dead.

He also said ... what does that mean you should do? Then you should be preparing. You should be seeking the will of God and focusing on that which is above and not on the things of this earth that will disappear in a fire.

We should all take to the streets and march against our common enemy who has hid in the shadows for too long. March in solidarity as one nation under God... saying to the devil–depart from this society, you are no longer welcome here. We will not believe your lies any longer. The lies that tell us because we're not wealthy we're not as worthy or as important as those who are or because we come from a certain neighborhood or ethnic group we're destined to be oppressed and not have as good a life as others. The lie that says because someone used to be addicted to drugs or has been in jail, that they don't deserve compassion, mercy a helping hand, to be seen as a person God loves.

> *"Philip found Nathaniel and said to him, "We have found Him of whom Moses in the law, and also the prophets, wrote – Jesus of Nazareth, the son of Joseph." And Nathaniel said to him, "Can anything good come out of Nazareth? Philip said to him, "Come and see." –* John 1:45-46

If Jesus Christ himself can come from a not so desirable neighborhood as this verse seems to demonstrate. Then if you are armed with the Holy Spirit and the Words of the Bible are engrained in your heart, then you can do amazing things too. No matter who you are, where you came from, or how old you are. Your Devine destiny awaits you.

> *"But the hour is coming, and now is, when the true worshipers will worship the Father in Spirit and truth; for the Father is seeking such to worship Him"* – John 4:23-24

Journal

- List of activities throughout your life that you love doing– that make you come alive with passion, purpose and a vibrancy that just makes you shine with excitement and joy.

- My Ideas:

How to Find the Path to Your Destiny

How to Find the Path to Your Destiny

How to Find the Path to Your Destiny

How to Find the Path to Your Destiny

Week of: _____

☐ Bliss from Growth ☐ Glory from Action ☐ Splendor from Achievement

_____

_____

_____

_____

_____

_____

_____

_____

_____

Exercise Performed this Week:

Week of: _____

☐ Bliss from Growth ☐ Glory from Action ☐ Splendor from Achievement

_____

_____

_____

_____

_____

_____

_____

_____

_____

Exercise Performed this Week:

Week of: _____

☐ Bliss from Growth ☐ Glory from Action ☐ Splendor from Achievement

_____

_____

_____

_____

_____

_____

_____

_____

_____

Exercise Performed this Week:

Week of: _____

☐ Bliss from Growth ☐ Glory from Action ☐ Splendor from Achievement

_____

_____

_____

_____

_____

_____

_____

_____

_____

_____

Exercise Performed this Week:

Week of: _____

☐ Bliss from Growth ☐ Glory from Action ☐ Splendor from Achievement

_____

_____

_____

_____

_____

_____

_____

_____

_____

Exercise Performed this Week:

Week of: _____

☐ Bliss from Growth ☐ Glory from Action ☐ Splendor from Achievement

_____

_____

_____

_____

_____

_____

_____

_____

_____

Exercise Performed this Week:

How to Find the Path to Your Destiny

Week of: _____

☐ Bliss from Growth ☐ Glory from Action ☐ Splendor from Achievement

_____

_____

_____

_____

_____

_____

_____

_____

Exercise Performed this Week:

Week of: _____

☐ Bliss from Growth ☐ Glory from Action ☐ Splendor from Achievement

_____

_____

_____

_____

_____

_____

_____

_____

_____

Exercise Performed this Week:

Week of: _____

☐ Bliss from Growth ☐ Glory from Action ☐ Splendor from Achievement

_____

_____

_____

_____

_____

_____

_____

_____

_____

Exercise Performed this Week:

Week of: _____

☐ Bliss from Growth ☐ Glory from Action ☐ Splendor from Achievement

_____

_____

_____

_____

_____

_____

_____

_____

_____

_____

Exercise Performed this Week:

Week of: _____

☐ Bliss from Growth ☐ Glory from Action ☐ Splendor from Achievement

_____

_____

_____

_____

_____

_____

_____

_____

_____

Exercise Performed this Week:

Week of: _____

☐ Bliss from Growth ☐ Glory from Action ☐ Splendor from Achievement

_____

_____

_____

_____

_____

_____

_____

_____

_____

_____

Exercise Performed this Week:

Week of: _____

☐ Bliss from Growth ☐ Glory from Action ☐ Splendor from Achievement

_____

_____

_____

_____

_____

_____

_____

_____

_____

Exercise Performed this Week:

Week of: _____

☐ Bliss from Growth ☐ Glory from Action ☐ Splendor from Achievement

_____
_____
_____
_____
_____
_____
_____
_____
_____

Exercise Performed this Week:

Week of: _____

☐ Bliss from Growth ☐ Glory from Action ☐ Splendor from Achievement

_____

_____

_____

_____

_____

_____

_____

_____

_____

Exercise Performed this Week:

Week of: _____

☐ Bliss from Growth ☐ Glory from Action ☐ Splendor from Achievement

_____

_____

_____

_____

_____

_____

_____

_____

_____

Exercise Performed this Week:

Week of: _____

☐ Bliss from Growth ☐ Glory from Action ☐ Splendor from Achievement

_____

_____

_____

_____

_____

_____

_____

_____

_____

Exercise Performed this Week:

Week of: _____

☐ Bliss from Growth ☐ Glory from Action ☐ Splendor from Achievement

_____

_____

_____

_____

_____

_____

_____

_____

_____

Exercise Performed this Week:

Week of: _____

☐ Bliss from Growth ☐ Glory from Action ☐ Splendor from Achievement

_____

_____

_____

_____

_____

_____

_____

_____

_____

Exercise Performed this Week:

Week of: _____

☐ Bliss from Growth ☐ Glory from Action ☐ Splendor from Achievement

_____

_____

_____

_____

_____

_____

_____

_____

_____

Exercise Performed this Week:

Week of: _____

☐ Bliss from Growth ☐ Glory from Action ☐ Splendor from Achievement

_____

_____

_____

_____

_____

_____

_____

_____

Exercise Performed this Week:

How to Find the Path to Your Destiny

Week of: _____

☐ Bliss from Growth ☐ Glory from Action ☐ Splendor from Achievement

_____

_____

_____

_____

_____

_____

_____

_____

_____

Exercise Performed this Week:

Week of: _____

☐ Bliss from Growth ☐ Glory from Action ☐ Splendor from Achievement

_____

_____

_____

_____

_____

_____

_____

_____

_____

Exercise Performed this Week:

Week of: _____

☐ Bliss from Growth ☐ Glory from Action ☐ Splendor from Achievement

_____

_____

_____

_____

_____

_____

_____

_____

_____

_____

Exercise Performed this Week:

Week of: _____

☐ Bliss from Growth ☐ Glory from Action ☐ Splendor from Achievement

_____

_____

_____

_____

_____

_____

_____

_____

Exercise Performed this Week:

Week of: _____

☐ Bliss from Growth ☐ Glory from Action ☐ Splendor from Achievement

_____

_____

_____

_____

_____

_____

_____

_____

_____

Exercise Performed this Week:

Week of: _____

☐ Bliss from Growth ☐ Glory from Action ☐ Splendor from Achievement

_____

_____

_____

_____

_____

_____

_____

_____

_____

Exercise Performed this Week:

How to Find the Path to Your Destiny

Week of: _____

☐ Bliss from Growth ☐ Glory from Action ☐ Splendor from Achievement

_____

_____

_____

_____

_____

_____

_____

_____

_____

_____

Exercise Performed this Week:

Week of: _____

☐ Bliss from Growth ☐ Glory from Action ☐ Splendor from Achievement

_____

_____

_____

_____

_____

_____

_____

_____

_____

Exercise Performed this Week:

Week of: _____

☐ Bliss from Growth ☐ Glory from Action ☐ Splendor from Achievement

_____

_____

_____

_____

_____

_____

_____

_____

_____

_____

Exercise Performed this Week:

How to Find the Path to Your Destiny

Week of: _____

☐ Bliss from Growth ☐ Glory from Action ☐ Splendor from Achievement

_____

_____

_____

_____

_____

_____

_____

_____

_____

Exercise Performed this Week:

Week of: _____

☐ Bliss from Growth ☐ Glory from Action ☐ Splendor from Achievement

_____

_____

_____

_____

_____

_____

_____

_____

_____

Exercise Performed this Week:

Week of: _____

☐ Bliss from Growth ☐ Glory from Action ☐ Splendor from Achievement

_____

_____

_____

_____

_____

_____

_____

_____

_____

Exercise Performed this Week:

How to Find the Path to Your Destiny

Week of: _____

☐ Bliss from Growth ☐ Glory from Action ☐ Splendor from Achievement

_____

_____

_____

_____

_____

_____

_____

_____

_____

_____

Exercise Performed this Week:

Week of: _____

☐ Bliss from Growth ☐ Glory from Action ☐ Splendor from Achievement

_____

_____

_____

_____

_____

_____

_____

_____

_____

Exercise Performed this Week:

Week of: _____

☐ Bliss from Growth ☐ Glory from Action ☐ Splendor from Achievement

_____

_____

_____

_____

_____

_____

_____

_____

_____

Exercise Performed this Week:

Week of: _____

☐ Bliss from Growth ☐ Glory from Action ☐ Splendor from Achievement

_____

_____

_____

_____

_____

_____

_____

_____

_____

Exercise Performed this Week:

Week of: _____

☐ Bliss from Growth ☐ Glory from Action ☐ Splendor from Achievement

_____

_____

_____

_____

_____

_____

_____

_____

_____

_____

Exercise Performed this Week:

Week of: _____

☐ Bliss from Growth ☐ Glory from Action ☐ Splendor from Achievement

_____

_____

_____

_____

_____

_____

_____

_____

_____

Exercise Performed this Week:

How to Find the Path to Your Destiny

Week of: _____

☐ Bliss from Growth ☐ Glory from Action ☐ Splendor from Achievement

_____

_____

_____

_____

_____

_____

_____

_____

_____

Exercise Performed this Week:

Week of: _____

☐ Bliss from Growth ☐ Glory from Action ☐ Splendor from Achievement

_____

_____

_____

_____

_____

_____

_____

_____

_____

Exercise Performed this Week:

Week of: _____

☐ Bliss from Growth ☐ Glory from Action ☐ Splendor from Achievement

_____

_____

_____

_____

_____

_____

_____

_____

_____

_____

Exercise Performed this Week:

- My favorite Bible Verses, quotes and notes about the Bible:

How to Find the Path to Your Destiny

How to Find the Path to Your Destiny

How to Find the Path to Your Destiny

How to Find the Path to Your Destiny

How to Find the Path to Your Destiny

How to Find the Path to Your Destiny

How to Find the Path to Your Destiny